I0082430

Pixelated Souls: An Intersection of Technology, Psychology, and Human Instinct

Abhinav Gaurav

Pixelated Souls
An Intersection of Technology, Psychology, and Human Instinct

Copyright © *Abhinav Gaurav,* 2025
All Rights Reserved

This book is subject to the condition that no part of this book is to be reproduced, transmitted in any form or means; electronic or mechanical, stored in a retrieval system, photocopied, recorded, scanned, or otherwise. Any of these actions require the proper written permission of the author.

Contents

Preface

Mahatma Gandhi once said, *"There is more to life than increasing its speed."* And honestly, that feels so relevant today. It's so easy to get caught up in the rush—always chasing more, faster, quicker. Everywhere I look, it's the same race.

But in this endless sprint, are we really living? Or just drifting further from who we truly are? Isn't it our ability to tell stories, share experiences, empathise, and create that makes us human?

In many ways, technology plays a huge role in this fast-paced mindset. The very tools and services designed to make life easier and more efficient have changed how we experience daily life. Today, our thoughts and actions move faster than ever—often without us even noticing.

Technology is a tricky thing. It doesn't change everything overnight—it sneaks in slowly, shaping our lives in ways we barely notice. Most of the time, though, it makes us believe it's improving our lives by helping us get things done more easily and at the speed needed to keep up with today's demands.

On top of that, the desire for instant gratification — getting what we want, when we want, and how we want — has most definitely reshaped our expectations and made us more dependent, little by little.

It was only after engaging in a few recent discussions with close friends and family that I began to realise just how deeply ingrained our dependence on digital devices has become and how effortlessly this dependency can take root in our lives. This realisation was the main reason I decided to write this book.

Here, I seek to explore the positive, negative, and often complex facets of technology, with the aim of raising awareness. It is my hope to foster a deeper understanding of the pivotal role we play in this intricate relationship while also highlighting the immense power we wield in shaping its direction.

As active participants in this ever-evolving digital revolution, we must resist the urge to be mere spectators. Instead, we need to step forward as contributors, actively shaping the landscape as it takes form. That is precisely what I set out to do here: to offer a clear view of what is unfolding, ignite awareness, and encourage deeper engagement in shaping the future of our digital world.

Here, I explore how technological advancements have shaped us as humans, enhancing certain aspects of our lives while also introducing new challenges. By closely examining these changes, I delve into their impact on areas such as cognitive growth, social relationships, and the trust we place in one another.

In this work, I explore the complex relationship between technology and the human mind, asking key questions:

- What impact does it have on how we communicate?

- How does technology shape the way we build our identities?

- And how does it influence our sense of self in today's digital world?

The goal here is not only to understand how technology shapes our thoughts and actions but also to challenge all of us — whether we're everyday users, researchers, or policymakers — to step back and critically reflect on the profound role technology plays in shaping our society.

Today, I truly believe it's vital for us to recognise our individual responsibility in navigating this complex digital world. This isn't just an abstract or academic debate — it's an urgent call to action. My hope is to inspire each of us to step up as stewards of the digital future, shaping technological progress with thoughtfulness and responsibility.

It is my belief that together, we have the power to harness these innovations for the greater good, ensuring that technology enriches our shared humanity rather than diminishes it. In a world where digital advancements evolve at a relentless pace, it's easy to feel like mere spectators, watching the game unfold beyond our control. But we are not just on the sidelines; we are players on the field, and it's up to us to take control of the game — shaping our lives, our relationships, and our well-being with intention and purpose.

My sincere hope is that readers walk away from this work not only with a deeper understanding of how technology impacts us but also with a renewed sense of ownership — a motivation to take charge of the digital future we are creating. A future where technology is not a source of distraction, disconnection, or imbalance but a force that nurtures genuine human connection, strengthens both body and mind, and fosters mutual respect.

I start by dedicating this poem to all of us.

Oh, how we love our glowing screens,
Where real life fades and fantasy gleams.
We talk to machines, they know our name,
As if that's normal - oh, what a game!

We're so connected, yet all alone,
Staring at faces that aren't our own.
We send our love with a heart emoji,
Because real affections just too soggy.

Connections made through apps thin,
Yet deeper bonds grow cold within.
But who are we behind the screen,
A fleeting thought, a filtered dream?

From social feeds to endless scrolls,
We give our time, our hearts, our souls.
Are we the same in flesh and wire?
Do our minds still burn with the same fire?

In this vast sea of pixels bright,
Do we remember what is right?
Or in the depths of cyberspace,
Do we sometimes lose our human grace?

In the world we build with virtual keys,
Let's not forget what it means to be free.
For while we're bound in the web we weave,
It's the human instinct that we must believe.

Introduction

Gone are the days when culinary creativity depended solely on our imagination. Today, our AI enabled fridge suggests mouth-watering recipes based on the ingredients we have at hand. Household chores, once tedious and time-consuming, are increasingly delegated to our robotic assistants. Even our health and fitness journeys have become personalised experiences, with intelligent algorithms guiding us according to our unique needs and goals. Just the other day, my friend took me to an AI-enabled gym where the equipment adapts to your body and fitness level, offering real-time feedback and custom workouts. Despite my tech background, it still felt like stepping into a different world.

In a world where our daily lives are more interconnected than ever—woven together by screens, digital platforms, and virtual interactions—I find myself deeply reflecting on the idea of a 'pixelated soul.' It feels like a powerful metaphor for how our existence has evolved in this digital age. More and more, I see how the human spirit feels fragmented into pixels, caught in an endless cycle of connection and isolation, creativity and consumption, constantly shifting between feeling seen and feeling lost in the noise.

This concept also speaks to something I've often felt—the tension between our physical, tangible selves and the carefully curated digital personas we present to the world. The 'pixelated soul' paints a vivid picture of this struggle, where our thoughts, emotions, and experiences are constantly broken apart and reshaped within the vibrant yet often chaotic realm of pixels and bytes that define our everyday interactions.

The digital revolution promised us freedom—boundless, limitless, overflowing with opportunities and creativity. It assured us that we could connect across vast distances, access a universe of knowledge at our fingertips, and step into worlds that once existed only in our imagination. It painted a vision where technology would empower us, amplifying our voices, expanding our possibilities, and redefining what it means to be human.

But no one told us that this digital utopia would come with a catch: to be part of it, we had to upload pieces of ourselves into the grid. Social media profiles and digital spaces stopped being just tools; they became extensions of who we are. Over time, these digital reflections didn't just influence how others saw us — they began to shape how we saw ourselves, blurring the lines between the reel and the real.

Today, our pixelated souls are scattered across countless digital spaces — Facebook, Alexa, Siri, LinkedIn, gaming platforms, chatbots, and more — while our devices are the constant portals pulling us into these worlds.

Modern technology, from smartphones to smartwatches, pushes us to refine and redesign how we show up — or even how we express ourselves — in the world, breaking the richness of human experience into bite-sized, digestible fragments. We walk when our watch tells us to. We drink when our phone beeps. Our lives, once guided by instinct and spontaneity, are now nudged, tracked, and optimised by algorithms.

Yet, in all this, something profound is lost. This fragmentation creates a deep sense of disconnection from self. The constant pressure to project perfection breeds anxiety, depression, and a loss of authenticity. The more we invest in our digital selves, the harder it becomes to reconcile them with our true, imperfect humanity. The line between engagement and addiction starts to blur. This is where technology begins to exploit our vulnerabilities. The pursuit of continuous interaction, instant convenience, and engaging experiences becomes a cycle of dependency, leaving us more entangled and detached from reality.

Technology gives the illusion of limitless freedom, yet it often traps us in invisible cages. Notifications, emails, and algorithms constantly pull at our attention, leaving little room for deep reflection or meaningful thought. We scroll endlessly through curated feeds, and slowly, our devices and algorithms start acting as modern jailers, trapping our pixelated souls.

As we pour more of ourselves into the digital world, our connection to the physical world diminishes. Moments once rich with family dinners are now disrupted by the glow of smartphones. Serene walks in nature are interrupted by the relentless buzz of notifications. And heartfelt conversations, even when challenging or emotionally charged, are overshadowed by our ever-present temptation to escape into the digital void.

While these momentary distractions may ease conflicts or create the illusion of smoothness, they ultimately weaken the depth and authenticity of human connection.

Even our creativity, one of the most quintessentially human traits, is increasingly mediated by technology. Artists rely on digital tools to create, musicians depend on algorithms to reach audiences, and even something as personal as writing a résumé is shaped by software suggesting what's most commercially appealing. While these tools open up new possibilities, they often prioritise ease and efficiency over authenticity, subtly steering creativity toward what is marketable rather than what is deeply personal or original.

This shift has diluted the human creative process. Just as audiences favour catchy, polished performances over raw, heartfelt expression, employers today seem more impressed by sleek, algorithmically optimised resumes than genuine authenticity.

But this mindset doesn't just shape job applications or creativity—it reshapes our perceptions and social norms, prioritising mass appeal over true self-expression and innovation, steering creativity toward what sells rather than what speaks to the soul.

So I ask, is this the world we want to create?

A world where external beauty takes precedence over the depth of our souls? Where readability outweigh authenticity? Where we choose conformity over individuality? Where fleeting impressions matter more than genuine, lasting connections? Where the pursuit of genuine love is constantly at odds with the ease of endless distractions?

Perhaps not. Perhaps we yearn for something deeper - a world where authenticity triumphs, where connection goes beyond the surface, and where love isn't diluted by convenience but strengthened by intention.

We often forget that being human means being imperfect—something my friends always remind me! But hey, I'm learning to embrace my flaws.

From the moment we are born, we are fraught with flaws—physical, emotional, and cognitive. Our bodies are vulnerable to disease, our minds susceptible to biases, and our societies prone to failure. Yet, despite this, the human pursuit of perfection has remained steadfast.

It is this drive that has propelled us to build towering cities, explore distant galaxies, and develop medical breakthroughs. It is why we created technology to make life easier, faster, and more efficient. But as technology progresses, our understanding of perfection has shifted. In fact, we are reaching a point where the quest for perfection is leading to dangerous outcomes, especially when we attempt to impose the flawless logic of machines onto the inherently imperfect nature of human life. Increasing reliance on algorithms and automation is blurring the messy, nuanced reality of human existence. As society grows more dependent on technological systems, we continue to lose touch with the qualities that make us human—creativity, empathy, intuition, and the ability to learn from our failures.

While technological tools expand possibilities, they also reshape the creative process, often placing marketability over authenticity. Human imperfection is not a flaw but an essential aspect of what makes us who we are. Technology, while offering glimpses of perfection, should not be seen as a remedy for our flaws. Instead, it should be a tool to help us navigate and cope with the challenges of living in an imperfect world. The interplay between our human imperfections and the perfection of technology may hold the key to creating a future that is both efficient and humane.

One of the most subtle yet damaging aspects of our digital existence is the illusion of control.

We believe we are the ones shaping our online personas, but in reality, the platforms that host them—social media networks, gaming ecosystems, and digital environments—are shaping us. Technology firms collect vast amounts of data, tailoring experiences to maximise engagement and profit. Our desires, fears, and habits are not just collected but meticulously analysed, monetised, and manipulated. In this digital cage, our pixelated selves are not only confined—they are commodified to serve corporate interests.

As we navigate the complexities of today's digital landscape, filled with immersive virtual reality and rapid advancements, the boundaries separating our online and offline worlds are becoming increasingly blurred, merging into a seamless tapestry of interaction and engagement. What was once confined to the realm of science fiction is now an everyday part of our reality.

Here, the fascinating field of Digital Psychology comes into play, offering a lens through which we can better understand ourselves and our interactions.

Digital Psychology examines how technology shapes our emotions, behaviours, and social interactions, helping us understand how we adapt to an ever-evolving digital landscape. By engaging with Digital Psychology, we can cultivate personal growth and self-awareness, enabling us to navigate the complex interplay between our digital experiences and authentic selves as we continually redefine our place in this technology-driven world.

As a psychology enthusiast, I am fascinated by the ongoing evolution of this field, which is undergoing a remarkable transformation. It is rare to witness the emergence of a new sub-discipline within psychology that not only develops so rapidly but also exerts such a profound impact, as this one has over the past two decades.

In today's digital era, understanding the profound ways technology shapes our minds and behaviours is both empowering and essential. This knowledge goes beyond academia or professional contexts – it is a vital tool for anyone seeking to lead a balanced and mindful life amidst the whirlwind of constant change.

The fusion of digital and physical spaces is more than just an evolution; it is a revolutionary shift, fundamentally transforming how we connect, create, and navigate our daily lives. But this transformation raises a critical question:

Are we unwittingly becoming digitally enslaved in a world intricately tied to our devices and online presence? In our pursuit of ease, control, convenience, and growth, are we risking the compromise of basic human values, creativity, and our sense of self?

In today's always-on, always-plugged-in, and always-presenting-and-pretending world, I believe it's entirely possible.

But if technology is merely an extension of human capability, shouldn't the idea of 'digital enslavement' ultimately come down to our own societal and individual choices? Or have we become so deeply entangled in this web of algorithms and connectivity that even the choices we believe are ours… aren't truly ours at all?

Devices should serve us, not control us: a belief most of us share. Yet, from the moment we wake up to the second we fall asleep, we are surrounded by screens, apps, and systems that quietly shape our daily lives.

What started as tools for convenience have now become constant companions, influencing not just how we interact with the world but how we think, feel, and even relate to ourselves. **But at what cost?**

Technology has undeniably changed our behaviours. In many ways, it has made life easier —

we can manage finances, shop, plan holidays, and even socialise (who can forget those endless Zoom calls during Covid?) without leaving our homes. It has redefined human connection: people who once feared loneliness after the end of a long marriage can now find companionship online, and niche communities have flourished, bringing like-minded individuals together. For some, the digital world has become a space to build social capital that feels out of reach offline.

But there's another side to this transformation. Our attention spans are shrinking, the depth of our relationships is changing, and a constant flood of digital interactions is making society more anxious, reactive, and, at times, aggressively disconnected from real human connection.

These examples raise more questions than any single book can answer. Thus, I have focused on a few key topics currently under study and research. The challenge of our time is to reclaim our humanity in an increasingly digital world. By recognising the traps and choosing paths that honour our spirit, we might transform our pixelated existence into something truly meaningful.

Will we remain trapped in the grid, or will we find a way to set our souls free? The answer doesn't lie in the technology we use but in the choices we make. True freedom begins with a conscious, intentional approach to technology — a mindset that prioritises purpose over impulse and wisdom over convenience.

Technology isn't inherently oppressive; it's a double-edged sword, capable of empowerment or harm. Its impact lies in how we wield it. So, I say, let's take charge of our digital relationship and transform it from a cage into a canvas — a space where creativity, connection, and humanity thrive.

The Evolution of Technology

We have indeed come a long way, and it is truly awe-inspiring to witness the remarkable evolution of technology. In just a few years of gradual progress, we have reached the stunning pinnacle of achievement—from the first stone tools to the rise of artificial intelligence (AI)—all driven by our desire to solve problems, improve efficiency, and push boundaries. This rapid evolution reflects our unyielding ambition to overcome limitations, explore new frontiers, and shape a future where the boundaries of possibility are constantly expanding. However, with these advancements come new challenges and ethical questions that invite us to reconsider the direction of our progress and the impact it has on humanity.

In this chapter, I will explore the rise of technology, tracing its evolution from the simplest tools used by our ancestors to the highly advanced systems we rely on today. I will examine the motivations behind these advancements, the societal needs that prompted their development, and how each innovation has influenced human behaviour. At times, I will also explain how, in our eagerness to remain at the forefront of innovation, we have often found ourselves entangled in a race to advance without fully considering the potential repercussions of our actions.

The concept of technology is ancient. As humans began to evolve, so did technology. It may not have been recognised in the same way as it is today, but there are countless references to advanced technologies, practices, and ideologies that laid the groundwork for human understanding of science and innovation in Hindu scriptures like the Vedas and Upanishads. These texts explore topics related to cosmology, medicine, and mathematics. These ancient scriptures often depict gods and sages with extraordinary knowledge and capabilities — ranging from flying vehicles called "Vimanas" (or aeroplanes) to advanced medicinal practices like Ayurveda. The Mahabharata and Ramayana, two of the most prominent epics in Hinduism, also describe technologies beyond the capabilities of the time, such as the use of powerful weapons, like the Brahmastra (a weapon of mass destruction).

These references to technology, while mythological, suggest that even the ancient worldview acknowledged the potential for human innovation. But there was also an inherent understanding that such advancements, when misused, could lead to devastation. Whether in the Vedic knowledge or the epic narratives, there was a constant recognition that humans needed to act with responsibility, morality, and wisdom when handling powerful tools such as technology.

With human evolution came the creation of simple tools, like stone axes, and the discovery of fire. Though basic, these tools gave early humans an edge over other species. They weren't just inventions but extensions of human abilities — designed to improve survival, ease labour, and expand possibilities. Early humans also learned to work together, share knowledge, and improve their skills, setting the stage for culture and civilisation. Civilisation itself came from social behaviours that went beyond just surviving. Back then, people probably lived in small groups, focused on finding food, staying safe, and raising their young. But once they discovered basic technology — fire, weapons, and tools — societies started taking shape.

Even clothing likely emerged around 100,000 years ago as humans adapted to colder climates. Early garments were probably simple coverings made from animal hides or plant fibres. But with the development of needles, bone awls, and other tools, humans began crafting more elaborate clothing for better protection against the elements.

Over time, clothing became more than just a necessity — it became a symbol of identity, social status, and culture, with different groups developing their own unique styles and techniques. This growing sense of identity and adaptation paved the way for even greater transformations in human society.

Around 10,000 BCE, the Agricultural Revolution marked a significant turning point in history. Humans transitioned from nomadic hunting and gathering to settled farming, fundamentally reshaping the way of life. This shift led to the development of new tools like ploughs and irrigation systems, increasing agricultural efficiency and allowing societies to grow larger and more complex.

The ability to cultivate crops and domesticate animals not only ensured a more stable food supply but also led to the formation of permanent settlements. As villages and towns emerged, organised social structures took shape—complete with laws, systems of trade, and cultural traditions—laying the foundation for the societies we know today.

However, for me, it was the Industrial Revolution of the 18th and 19th centuries stands out as one of the biggest turning points in history, introducing innovations such as the steam engine, textile machinery, and electricity. Mechanisation, a key feature of this revolution, not only increased productivity but also redefined social structures and lifestyles. The Industrial Revolution led to the creation of the modern factory system, rapid urbanisation, and significant social and economic changes. Early humans created art and tools, but they were more for their own survival. But with the industrial revolution, humans learned to earn from their creations. Metalworking technologies allowed for the production of better tools and weapons.

As humans began to form more complex social structures—moving from small groups of hunter-gatherers to larger agricultural societies—their needs expanded beyond the essentials of survival. The development of language, culture, and cooperation allowed humans to share resources, form social bonds, and work together for mutual benefit. This, in turn, led to a shift from mere survival to the pursuit of comfort, status, and security within the group.

Human history is a story of progress, driven by our endless desire for more — more comfort, more control, more power, more wealth. In the beginning, our needs were tied to survival. But as societies advanced, the pursuit of progress gradually shifted. What once drove us forward with purpose turned into an urge to compete, and the drive for growth became a craving for comfort.

This transformation reached new heights in the 20th and 21st centuries with an unprecedented information revolution. The rise of computers, smartphones, and the rapid spread of the internet ushered in the digital age — where progress was no longer just about physical expansion or industrial achievement, but about the control and commodification of information itself.

I came across an interesting Hindi phrase that stuck with me: "*Pehle bhagwan deta tha; aaj data bhagwan hai.*" Loosely translated, it means: *God once gave with love and grace; today, data decides the time and place.* Funny, yet deeply thought-provoking! It's a powerful reflection of the world today - where data doesn't just inform but subtly steers what we see, shapes what we believe, and influences who we become.

Beyond progress, the 20th and 21st centuries also ushered in an era of warfare, environmental destruction, and societal upheaval, revealing the double-edged nature of technological advancement. The very innovations that propelled us forward cast a long shadow over humanity's ability to wield its newfound power responsibly. The Information Age, driven by the rise of computers and the internet, transformed society on an unprecedented scale. Yet, as we eagerly embraced innovation, it became alarmingly clear that technology was advancing faster than our capacity to wield it ethically.

The internet revolutionised communication, enabling instant global connectivity, but also introduced darker phenomena—manipulation, surveillance, and rampant misinformation. Social media emerged as a powerful tool for connection, yet it also became a breeding ground for hate, division, and widespread anxiety, reflecting both the promise and peril of our digital age.

Today, we are witnessing advancements that once seemed unimaginable. Nanotechnology, biotechnology, and space exploration are rapidly reshaping our world. We are sending humans to Mars, engineering custom genetic material, and developing ever-more intelligent machines.

But it's clear that the same technologies with the power to elevate human life also raise serious ethical and societal concerns. AI, for example, is set to revolutionise industries, yet it brings fears of mass surveillance, the erosion of privacy, and the rise of deepfake technology, blurring the lines between reality and deception.

Climate change and environmental degradation are among the biggest challenges we face today, largely driven by our unsustainable use of technology. Centuries of rapid industrialisation have led to pollution, resource depletion, and global warming—threats that put the very survival of our planet at risk.

So, it's fair to say that while we've made incredible technological advances, we've failed to apply the same level of innovation to solving the existential crises we now face. I can't help but wonder — how did we become so good at creating problems and then finding ways to create even more out of them?

We stand at a pivotal moment today. On one hand, technology offers extraordinary benefits, unlocking new possibilities and streamlining tasks in ways we never imagined. On the other, our growing dependence on these innovations has shifted them from necessities to compulsions, introducing significant challenges we can no longer ignore.

The relentless pace of digital advancement shows no signs of slowing, and humanity's insatiable curiosity continues to propel us into the vast landscape of emerging technologies — pushing us further into uncharted territory.

Humans have a natural inclination toward immediate rewards and solutions, a tendency deeply rooted in our evolutionary psychology. The human mind is inherently designed to be lazy — a survival mechanism that helps conserve energy in the face of scarcity. This bias towards short-term benefits often takes precedence over long-term consequences, particularly when it comes to technological innovation.

This is why one of the most crucial aspects of technology's evolution is the need for thoughtful regulation and ethical guidelines. While individual mindfulness plays a key role, it's not enough on its own — governments, businesses, and scientists must also work together to ensure that technological advancements are developed and deployed responsibly. This means creating policies that tackle issues like data privacy, the ethical use of AI, and the environmental impact of new innovations.

I have explored a few ideas later in this book, including the need for an independent, unbiased body to regulate technological advancement — one that prioritises ethics, fairness, and the well-being of society over profit and power.

The story of technology reveals a pattern. Humanity has often been caught in the rush to modernise without fully considering the ethical, environmental, and societal consequences of its innovations. From the wisdom of Hindu scriptures to the technological marvels of the modern age, one truth remains: technology is neither inherently good nor evil; it is a tool. Its impact on the world depends on how we choose to use it. In ancient texts, we see that even the gods and sages could not always avoid the consequences of misused power.

Today, as we stand at the threshold of new technological frontiers, it is crucial to remember that we must wield our tools with wisdom, responsibility, and a deep commitment to the well-being of all. Technology must remain a tool that helps us solve problems, stay connected, and be productive, not an addiction that detracts from our well-being or relationships. Most importantly, it must never replace what truly makes us human.

It's critical to understand that in the race to become more modern, we never lose sight of our moral compass, guided by the ancient wisdom that once cautioned us about the dangers of unchecked power.

The digital age was born out of necessity, a response to humanity's growing need for connection, efficiency, and progress. It has given us unprecedented tools to shape our lives and the world. So, the question today is not to reject technology, but to reclaim it—harnessing its potential while mitigating its harms. This paradox is not a flaw of technology itself but of how it is designed, deployed, and used.

Perhaps by looking a little deeper at how technology has changed our behaviours, we can reclaim our autonomy and ensure that it remains a positive force in our lives.

Changing Human Behaviour

Imagine stepping out the door each morning. What three things would you grab without a second thought? Not long ago, the answer would have been simple: "wallet," "watch," and "keys" — practical and essential.

But times have changed. Today, one item stands above all the rest, something we feel almost incomplete without: our *smartphone*. A 2021 study showed that the average person checks their phone over 96 times a day — once every ten minutes. Our ancestors may have relied on gut instinct to sense danger, but today, our phone is our lifeline.

Love it or loathe it, the smartphone has evolved into an indispensable tool, seamlessly integrating itself into nearly every aspect of our lives. It keeps us connected, guides us with navigation, entertains us, and organises our daily schedules. Leaving home without one feels almost unthinkable, triggering a deep sense of unease, as if we are stepping out unprepared, stripped of safety, convenience, and our vital link to the world. The smartphone has become an extension of us, transforming the way we interact with the modern world.

Throughout history, we've relied on connections to survive and thrive. Human need to connect is deeply rooted in our biology, psychology, and even our survival instincts. So it's not a surprise that, today, we pride ourselves on being more connected than ever before.

With a few taps, we can communicate with anyone around the world, access a seemingly infinite amount of information, and even manage our lives from the palm of our hand. Yet, we cannot deny the fact that today many of our "connections" remain shallow and transactional. It is ironic that the more we "connect" today, the more disconnected we become from real human interaction and, ultimately, from ourselves.

And communication is not the only way technology is changing our behaviour.

Imagine this:

With the first rays of sunlight filter through the curtains, a person wakes up and calls out, "What's the weather today?" bypassing the usual human instinct to glance outside at the sky. Next, ask to play a favourite music, set a crucial reminder, or gather a comprehensive briefing of the day's events.

A clear change in our behaviours.

We're anthropomorphising our homes and objects - giving them a "voice" and treating them like companions, asking things like "Alexa, what's the weather today?" or "Hey Siri, play my favourite song." Many of us today talk to our homes in a way that was once regarded as bizarre, rude, or impersonal. It's a strange new way humans have learned to communicate.

Once seen as everyday routines, these tasks required tangible, physical or mental engagement -

whether interacting with a human being or using one's own sensory inputs. Today, they've shifted to verbal exchanges with a machine. Almost as if we've trained ourselves to engage more with machines than other humans or rely on our mental abilities for certain tasks. The worst part is we are not done yet. With every passing day, we are moving away from our human creativity and intelligence and choosing to be closer to machines.

The rise of new devices, robots, cars, and virtual worlds has changed how we think, act, and express ourselves. We don't need to think too far—I can take my own example of how the devices around us are changing our behaviours without realisation. There was a time when manual toothbrushes were normal in households, and I was accustomed to using one. In the last 10 years or so, as I have gotten used to using an electric toothbrush, I can't even imagine using a manual one again—a clear example of how technology is changing our basic behaviour and, in some cases, even our skills.

Question: How many of us today can park a car without parking assistance?

Human behaviour is an array of actions and reactions exhibited by individuals, influenced by internal processes, external stimuli, and environmental contexts. It is a complex interplay of biological, psychological, and social factors shaped by individual experiences and cognitive processes. Throughout history, our behaviours have been shaped by a variety of factors, from survival instincts to social norms to the advancements in technology. Recent years have witnessed a rapid shift in how humans interact with both - themselves and other humans. Our perception and approach to the world has changed. The factors driving these changes are intricate, but two of the most influential forces are technological advancements and shifts in societal values. These forces are not only altering how we behave but are also reshaping our identities and cognitive processes.

Here are some key ways human behaviours are changing in today's world.

Communications

The rapid evolution of technology over the past few decades has significantly reshaped how people communicate, interact, and form relationships. Technological communication has transformed human behaviour from early childhood to adulthood and within various social contexts, such as interpersonal relationships and the workplace. Before the digital era, communication was predominantly face-to-face or conducted through written letters. Today, messaging apps and online tools have revolutionised how people connect. Children and adolescents, in particular, have embraced social media platforms, texting, and instant messaging as their preferred means of communication. While this has bridged long distances, it has also led to a decline in interpersonal interactions. For many, this stunts social development and hinders the acquisition of non-verbal communication skills like reading body language or interpreting emotions.

One of the most immediate and noticeable impacts of technological communication is the shift toward instant gratification. With a few taps, people can send messages, share photos, or even video chat with others around the world. Unlike traditional forms of communication such as letters or phone calls, digital communication allows for near-instantaneous connection, making people accustomed to quick responses. The ability to communicate in real-time has reduced the barriers of distance and time, but has led to a reduction in patience. People now expect faster replies, whether in personal or professional settings. If responses are delayed, frustration can build, often leading to misunderstandings or anxiety. Digital communication also fosters a constant influx of messages. This has led to new behaviours such as an "always-on" culture and digital burnout.

Learning & Development

The landscape of learning and development has also undergone a dramatic transformation with the advent of technological communication. In recent decades, digital tools and platforms have changed how we acquire knowledge, collaborate, and share information. This shift in communication has not only impacted the way we learn but also the behaviours and skills required in the workplace and education systems.

With the wealth of information available on the internet, individuals now have the freedom to access learning materials anytime, anywhere. Platforms like Coursera and YouTube provide courses and tutorials on virtually any subject, empowering individuals to take control of their learning journey. Online platforms have made education accessible to millions, breaking down traditional barriers like geography or cost. Learners have gained greater control over their learning journeys. Technology has fostered a shift from formal education to continuous, lifelong learning.

That said, the convenience of digital learning and the constant availability of information can also lead to information overload. With the flood of online content, learners may struggle to focus on one task or topic, constantly jumping between tabs, messages, and notifications. The overwhelming volume of accessible content can also lead to burnout or fatigue, especially when learners feel pressured to consume vast amounts of information to keep themselves ahead of others. As a result, technology has also given rise to the issue of shallow learning. Online platforms often provide bite-sized, surface-level content that may lack depth or fail to engage learners at a deeper cognitive level.

Learners skim through articles, watch short video clips, or complete quizzes without engaging in critical thinking or deeper reflection. This results in a superficial understanding of topics and can hinder long-term retention and application of knowledge.

Social Interactions

One of the most profound changes brought about by technological communication is the ability to connect with others across the globe. Platforms like Facebook, Twitter, Instagram, and LinkedIn enable individuals to stay in touch with friends, family, colleagues, and even strangers from different parts of the world, influencing everything from friendships to work. Technology has expanded the reach of social networks, allowing people to connect with a broader range of individuals, including distant friends, family members, and new professional connections

While technology has facilitated connections, it has also contributed to a sense of social isolation. Apps have transformed the meaning of connection and relationships, making it easier to meet potential people. Yet, this has also introduced swipe culture and superficial relationships with no emotional depth.

Many individuals use digital platforms as an escape from their real-world problems, opting to engage in superficial interactions rather than addressing the emotional or social needs. The ease of forming relationships has led to an emphasis on having more friends or followers rather than fostering deep, meaningful connections. People constantly update their online profiles or engage in surface-level conversations to maintain a certain image or to seek relationship, which, in turn, undermine authentic relationships.

The office communication that once primarily occurred through face-to-face meetings, phone calls, and written memos is now dominated by digital, instantaneous tools. Email, instant messaging, video conferences, and collaborative platforms like Despite being more connected than ever, technology is contributing to feelings of isolation. Our brains have adopted technology so much that many continue to live a virtual life, leading to a paradox of loneliness in a hyper-connected world. As work and social lives increasingly shift to online spaces, the depth of personal connections often diminishes, leaving individuals longing for more meaningful, face-to-face interactions. This digital shift, while offering convenience, often reduces the warmth and emotional depth that comes with in-person communication

Daily Routines

Technology has also played a crucial role in shaping our daily routines, offering unparalleled convenience while also encouraging over-dependency and reliance. Consider wearable technology like fitness trackers - they not only promote health awareness but can lead to an unhealthy obsession with tracking every metric. Online shopping and ready-food delivery have enhanced convenience but also have led to impulsive buying behaviours and reduced patience. The attractive pull of apps, games, and streaming platforms has contributed to increased screen time and a more sedentary lifestyle, undermining our physical well-being. Moreover, while AI and robotics are revolutionising our economy and society, they also raise pressing concerns about job loss and economic disparity that we must address.

Mind & Cognition

The influence of technology on human cognition is a crucial concern. Issues related to privacy and people's awareness of how their data is collected have become increasingly significant. Constant connectivity and the pressure to maintain digital personas have serious implications for mental health, contributing to anxiety, stress, and a fear of missing out.

The rapid evolution of technology has also altered societal values, prioritising efficiency and convenience over the time-honoured virtues of patience and perseverance. Today, many find themselves immersed in the online world for significant portions of their lives, a phenomenon that greatly influences their identities and self-perceptions. The quest for validation has taken on a formidable role as a driving force for many, impacting not only the sense of self-worth but also subtly directing daily behaviours and interactions, leading to a cycle of comparison and social engagement that shapes experiences and outlook on life.

The constant stream of information, updates, and content has significantly reduced our attention spans. Studies and expert opinions show that our ability to focus and sustain attention on tasks has been affected by various factors, including the rise of digital media, multitasking, and the fast-paced nature of modern life, with individuals often struggling to focus on tasks for extended periods.

This phenomenon is exacerbated by the addictive design of many technologies. Social media platforms use algorithms to maximise user engagement, often at the expense of productivity and mental well-being. The dopamine rush from likes, shares, and comments can lead to compulsive behaviour, creating a cycle of dependency. Technology has enhanced cognitive abilities in certain areas. Access to vast amounts of information online allows for quicker decision-making. Apps and digital tools have made complex tasks like language translation and data analysis more accessible to the average user. While these offer opportunities, they also promote isolation and a more sedentary, intellectually passive lifestyle.

Think about it!

Heading to a movie hall with family wasn't just an outing—it was an experience. The physical movement, the buzz of excitement, and the shared anticipation brought a unique energy that strengthened the bond. It wasn't just entertainment; it was about bringing that family feeling to life!

Today, we have apps for meditation, therapy, and mood tracking, providing accessible support for those in need. Wearable devices monitor physical health metrics, encouraging users to take charge of their own health. But ever thought, why did we require these in the first place? For those in need, I agree that technology has helped and should continue to help.

But for those for whom technology is merely a convenience, I say: **it's time to think**!

We have learned to distance ourselves from friends and family in the name of co-dependency, yet we proudly embrace it when it comes to our robots and technology. We hesitate to show vulnerability to those closest to us, fearing it makes us weak, yet we unquestioningly surrender to technology's creek. We feel anxious or lost without our smartphones, and we crave validation from social media. We shy away from seeking advice or emotional support from those closest to us, yet we instinctively turn to Google and apps for answers, often trusting them more than the people in our lives. It's ironic — what we resist in human relationships, we readily accept from machines.

In the coming days, by leveraging quantum mechanics, our computers promise to solve more problems that are currently intractable. Technologies like CRISPR gene editing and regenerative medicine could redefine human health and longevity. Companies like SpaceX and other agencies are investing heavily in colonising Mars and mining asteroids, making space the next frontier of technological exploration.

The relationship between technology and humans is not merely cyclical but reflects our evolution, continually shaping our minds. This underscores the need to protect our brain—our ultimate supercomputer.

The Ultimate Supercomputer

As ancient Indian philosophy puts it, *"The mind is more restless than the wind, swayed by the voices it has sinned."* It drifts, wavers, and sometimes gets tangled in the echoes of the past. No wonder we've spent centuries trying to understand it. At some point, we've all stared at our own reflection, lost in thought, and wondered: *What's really going on in there?* It's a question as old as self-awareness itself — a mystery that keeps pulling us back, daring us to figure it out.

We are constantly seeking to unravel the complexities of our thoughts, emotions, and actions, trying to decode how we perceive the world around us. But to truly understand how anything — including technology — impacts our minds, we must first grasp the intricate workings of the human brain. From the formation of memories to the process of decision-making, every function relies on this delicate interplay of neurons, chemicals, and electrical signals. Only by understanding these processes, perhaps, we can begin to see the true influence of technology on our cognitive landscape.

Every day, our brain processes about 70,000 thoughts, filtering what matters from the noise. When we see a face, our brain doesn't merely register visual features; it evaluates emotional expressions, recalls memories associated with that person, and even predicts how we should respond. This all happens almost instantaneously, with millions of neurons firing in parallel to create a coherent interpretation — much like a supercomputer running a complex simulation. From simple tasks to complex problem-solving, the brain's ability to organise, store, and retrieve information is nothing short of awe-inspiring. But how exactly does this process work?

Neuroscientists have gathered plenty of fascinating observations about the brain. Yet, despite the wealth of knowledge, the fundamental question persists: How do a collection of individual cells — neurons — combine to create intelligence, creativity, and the full theatre of consciousness?

The human brain remains one of the most fascinating enigmas in science, and at the heart of its complexity lies the neocortex. A so-called folded, six-layered sheet of neural tissue makes up the bulk of the cerebral cortex. The neocortex plays a vital role in numerous higher-order cognitive functions - like a supercomputer, organising and processing vast amounts of data to shape our experiences, including sensory perception, language processing, logical reasoning, and abstract thinking. Despite significant advances in neuroscience, the neocortex remains steeped in mystery, challenging researchers to unravel its full potential and purpose.

Allow me to share a fascinating analogy. Imagine the Neocortex, the part of our brain responsible for higher-order thinking, as being like one of my favourite dishes – Biryani.

Now, picture each grain of rice in the Biryani, each one separate yet part of a grander whole. Imagine laying them down one by one in neat, evenly spaced rows. On top of that, think of each grain being gently infused with layers of aromatic spices, giving them a subtle burst of flavour. Then, picture moist paneer (*I am vegetarian. Please feel free to imagine chicken*) nestled in between the grains, their juices slowly seeping into the rice, creating a rich, intricate pattern of textures. Now, imagine this process repeating over and over again – each layer building upon the last, creating a masterpiece of complexity. Just like the grains of rice and layers of spices in Biryani, the neurons in the Neocortex layer upon each other, connecting and interacting in a delicate balance.

The Neocortex, a shiny, overhyped part of the brain, is the secret spice behind all human intelligence. Everything we know or could know – every thought, sight, sound, or imagination we've ever experienced in our lives is stored here. It's this wrinkled, folded mass of the brain that occupies about 70% of the space inside our skull. The Neocortex is further divided into regions that process sensory input, motor functions, and complex associations

The term 'Neocortex,' meaning 'New Layer,' refers to its recent evolution. It wraps around older, more primitive parts of the brain, like the limbic system – the part we often call the "reptilian brain." Although those grains of Biryani – we can't see them individually with the naked eye - they come together to form something complex and intricate. In the same way, the Neocortex also look like one big, crinkly sheet on the surface, but beneath that, it's made up of countless tiny neurons, each connected in an elaborate, column-like structure.

This is how the Neocortex empowers us to experience the world: seeing vibrant colours, hearing melodies, feeling textures, and diving into deep reasoning. It's this remarkable structure that allows us to master languages, solve complex problems, form relationships, and even, for people like me, ponder philosophy.

Despite all the diverse tasks it handles, the Neocortex operates with a quiet, underlying harmony, much like the perfect balance of flavours in Biryani. But here's the intriguing puzzle – the human neocortex shares a compelling similarity with other mammals – creatures that may not speak languages, solve Rubik's cubes, or grasp quantum physics. So, how is it that this single type of brain tissue, known as the cortical column, contributes to such a vast array of cognitive and sensory functions?

The key to this puzzle lies in our human roots – our instincts and our predictive abilities. It's true. Despite all the technological advancements, our brain is nothing more than a sophisticated prediction machine.

Picture this:

A human organ – the brain – connected to nothing, lying in total isolation. Now hook this brain up to some sort of sensory input – say a visual feed from a camera somewhere (in human organ terms, these are our eyes), with a signal delivered by little spikes of neuron activation. The brain takes these signals, which are incomprehensible at first and begins detecting patterns. And then patterns of patterns. Soon enough, it starts to anticipate what will come next – start modelling and predicting the input the same way any supercomputer may run models forecasting the weather. Every time a prediction gets wrong, the brain updates this model a little bit, refining it to yield better predictions next time. That is, there are fewer surprises about what may come next.

Now, connect this brain to another sensory input – a couple of hands. With hands, our brain starts to learn about the world in a new way – by touching it and manipulating it. The brain now sees and holds an object – say, a stapler. It rotates this thing around, looking at it from all angles. It presses down on the thing, and a staple pops out. It pulls the thing open at the hinge and sees a hundred staples inside, all lined up in a neat row. Now, the brain isn't just passively waiting for data; it's actively creating it.

Heard of the phrase – *use it or lose it*! The phrase originated from the fact that the more we use our brain, the better it gets in predictions or, in other words, makes us more intelligent. The whole time, our brain uses the new data to create a better, more refined, more accurate model of the world around us. As humans – heck, as organisms – we model to survive. These models are crucial because they help us make predictions, and predictions give us control. For example, if I reach out, grab the doorknob, turn it clockwise, and pull, the door will open. Or if I'm nice to the person in front of me, they might smile and share their Tiramisu (*yes, it's my favourite dessert*) with me.

This is why our intelligence, at its core, is nothing more than the ability to create better models of the world, one tiny piece at a time, and use those models to navigate life and get things done. It's almost poetic when you think about it: the world we experience is essentially a simulation, a vivid hallucination running in our neocortex, constantly working to make sense of the chaotic and often strange reality outside. In that sense, we're all living in our own personal versions of the world, constructed by our brains. And this brings us to an uncomfortable truth—mental illness is just as normal as physical illness. The difference? Physical illnesses are easier for us to recognise. Our brain, after all, has a well-established model for the body and its ailments, so it's quicker to spot and label a fever, a broken bone, or a cough. But mental illness? That's where the challenge lies. Our brains are ill-equipped to model themselves, to truly grasp the turbulence of our thoughts and emotions.

Now that we've understood how human intelligence works, we can connect it to how technology, especially Artificial Intelligence, operates. Apps, games, and even online systems are designed to teach us, challenge our brains in ways that aren't natural, and stimulate neuroplasticity – the brain's ability to rewire itself when faced with new experiences. So, instead of learning through touch or the other natural senses our brain is familiar with, we're teaching our brains to learn through stimulation. But here's the catch:

stimulation is a double-edged sword. Relying too much on technology for memory or problem-solving can weaken the brain's natural ability to develop these skills on its own.

Studies have shown that too much screen time can change the way our brain works, especially in the prefrontal cortex, which controls our focus and impulse control. Imagine how we're constantly bombarded with the latest gossip, funny memes, or viral videos on social media. These platforms use smart algorithms to keep us glued to our screens with a never-ending flow of exciting content – *like that hilarious video where a cat is trying to catch its own tail for the tenth time* (you know, the one you couldn't stop watching and even forwarded to your friends). This constant stream of novelty and emotional highs can mess with how we manage our emotions and decision-making. It's like getting caught up in the chaos of a never-ending soap opera – the drama, the excitement, and the suspense, all at once. Over time, it does overwhelm our brain's circuits.

The relationship between technology and the Neocortex is as complex as a chess game played by the mind itself. On one hand, it opens doors to endless learning and creativity, offering unparalleled opportunities for growth. On the other, it comes with the risk of overstimulation, which can overload our mental circuits or develop habits that hold us back. Finding balance is like navigating a crowded Indian street in a city like Varanasi: full of potential, but requiring constant attention to avoid chaos.

Technology gives us powerful tools to expand the neocortex, enhancing our ability to think, create, and innovate. But ultimately, it's up to us to protect our most valuable asset: our minds — our ultimate supercomputer — from overclocking.

Overclocked Processor

There's an old Indian saying — *"Jitna tez bhaago, utni zyada saans phoolti hai."* Meaning, the faster you run, the more breathless you get. And isn't that exactly what is happening to our minds today? We're all racing at full speed, but the real question is — are we actually heading somewhere, or just desperately running away from ourselves? And for what? Stress, exhaustion, and the occasional mental breakdown. After all these years of evolution, is this really the best we can do?

It's almost like we've taken another old Indian saying — *"The harder the battle, the sweeter the victory"* — a little too literally. But instead of fighting real battles, we've turned our own minds into battlegrounds.

In a world where overthinking has practically become an Olympic sport, giving our minds a break has turned into a luxury reserved for the so-called "lazy" or "unproductive" ones. But is it really? Don't you think this constant hustle is slowly draining us, much like a drip-drip-drip from a leaky tap, wearing down even the toughest stone!

Imagine a computer that is never down and continually getting feeds, sometimes out of fear, at times out of curiosity, or, of course, out of necessity. That's our brain today - constantly absorbing inputs, rarely decompressing. We consume information at speeds that would have seemed impossible just decades ago, yet instead of feeling more aware, we feel more exhausted.

Every machine - whether a computer, car, factory assembly line, or a human brain - is designed to handle specific tasks within a certain capacity. When a machine is asked to perform beyond its limits - by processing too many instructions or by handling too much data - it begins to slow down or even break down. We might call this the "overload syndrome," the way we sometimes push ourselves, in the hope of keeping up with the relentless pace set by society – or more likely, the digital world we're now immersed in.

While the human brain is a remarkable organ capable of performing more complex tasks than any machine, it too can suffer from overload when bombarded with excessive information, especially from external stimuli. The ancient Indian concept of *Prana* — the vital energy — teaches us the importance of balance. Too much of anything, even information, disrupts this natural flow.

Let me give you an example. As I write this book, I've become so obsessed with it that I haven't slept for the past two nights. If I keep going like this, would that be healthy? Could I even survive? And more importantly, would I be able to finish my thoughts — or even finish the book itself?

Every obsession, no matter how healthy it seems, becomes a poisonous apple when taken to extremes.

I hear these arguments from many: "Oh, I only check my phones at certain times", or "I keep my notifications disabled. Not many of us realise that it's not just about the technology that is switched on; research shows that technology affects our mental health, cognitive functions, and overall brain health even when we're not actively engaging with devices.

In a way, it's like cooking food in a pressure cooker — the heat is still there, even if we're not the ones stirring or keeping an eye on it. The food cooks, but the pressure builds up, and it affects everything around it. Similarly, the constant presence of technology in our lives can "cook" our minds slowly, generating stress and impacting us physically and mentally, even when we're not consciously interacting with it. It's like that moment when we forget we're cooking biryani on the stove and suddenly, the whole kitchen smells like it's about to explode — except, in this case, it's our mind!

To understand this a little more, we need to understand our brain components and something called an EMF or the Electromagnetic Field.

An EMF (or the electromagnetic field) is created by any electrically charged object, and guess what? It's everywhere—even the Earth and our bodies generate them! Ever noticed how, during a power outage, everything goes silent, yet you still feel the pull of the Earth's energy? It's like the planet's way of saying, "I'm still here." Now, here's a fun fact: the human heart generates its own EMF, and the heart's EMF is about 60 times stronger than the brain's, detectable up to 3 feet away! This always makes me think about how in Indian culture, we often say two people are "vibing" with each other. It's that unspoken connection, as if their heart's EMFs are in sync—almost like they're communicating on a deeper level.

Although, thinking about it, my EMF must be in the negatives! No wonder I 'vibe' more with my favourite cup of chai than with people. Honestly, I probably end up making chai for others just so my heart's EMF doesn't get lonely!

Anyway. The point here is, human heart and brain are deeply interconnected, and the two EMFs together influence a person's mental state. Feelings like love, compassion, and gratitude create a more coherent, organised heart rhythm and relaxed feelings. Conversely, negative emotions such as stress, fear, or overstimulation can disrupt this, leading to a more chaotic biofield. When we speak of 'stress' in our Indian families, it's often tied to the idea that our energies are out of balance. Perhaps it's more of a spiritual concept, but it holds true in the physiological sense as well.

Technology today has become a constant source of electromagnetic pollution, exposing us to external radiation even when we're not actively using our phones, computers, or devices. This is why the mere presence of technology can have a lasting effect on our brains and our body's electromagnetic fields (EMFs).

Humans are designed to survive, instinctively prioritising any life-threatening situations. Our brain only deals with a problem when it reaches a point where our well-being is directly impacted. Our prefrontal cortex (PFC), a part of the neocortex, controls this. When we experience a situation, the neocortex helps process the information and decide how to respond by working with other brain structures, like the limbic system (which controls emotions) and the amygdala (which triggers the body's "fight-or-flight" response), prioritising any immediate life-threatening situation first.

Research reveals that constant exposure to unnatural EMFs from electronic devices can induce a persistent state of stress and heightened alertness. Even when we think we've stepped away, their effects linger, subtly influencing us beneath the surface. Unfortunately, our brains do not register this as an immediate threat. Instead, the cumulative stress builds over time, leading to what is known as 'A-typical burnout,' chronic stress, or a delayed response.

Many will recall experiencing this phenomenon during the COVID-19 pandemic, where individuals continued to feel the after-effects of the disease long after recovering from the initial symptoms. Even after testing negative and showing no signs of active infection, many reported lingering effects—fatigue, brain fog, and other persistent issues. This phenomenon, often referred to as a 'delayed response,' highlights how the body continue reacting long after the apparent threat has passed.

Over time, this stress can manifest as chronic body pain, gastrointestinal issues like acid reflux or IBS, and, in severe cases, even life-threatening conditions such as cancer—illustrating how the body keeps the score.

A-typical burnout doesn't always scream for attention—it is often sneaky, showing up in unexpected ways, as a delayed response. A-typical burnout may appear insignificant initially, the gradual nature of this condition highlights the urgency for immediate action to prevent its onset. And yet, in our society, we often dismiss it. In many countries and cultures, even today, mental health issues are usually downplayed, and the focus remains always on "hard work" and "perseverance." Recognising the reality of A-typical burnout, understanding its subtle signs, and addressing it early on can make all the difference in maintaining a healthy, balanced life and avoiding delayed stress response.

In today's technology-driven world, A-typical burnout has become increasingly common. It is simply because our neocortex is constantly dealing with immediate issues first – the environmental changes causing physical threats, such as viruses, job security, and many other day-to-day necessary activities – causing a constant fight or flight response. Our brain simply does not get a chance to adequately process the stress that arises from external sources, such as technology and devices, until it becomes a direct threat

The delayed response is not just a quirky feature of modern life; it's a biological reality that influences everything from our heart rate to our stress levels.

When we experience stress, the body releases cortisol, the primary stress hormone. However, it's not always the immediate cause of stress that affects us. The anticipation of a delayed response – like waiting for a critical email or wondering how someone will react to something you said – can also cause prolonged cortisol release, keeping our bodies in a state of tension. Our brains are constantly preparing for what's next, even if "what's next" isn't coming until tomorrow (or next week, depending on how much your friend really wants to make you wait).

When the body experiences stress, the fight-or-flight response kicks in, which increases heart rate and blood pressure. However, if the response to a stressful situation is delayed or prolonged, the body remains in this heightened state longer than necessary. This chronic strain can lead to the gradual wear and tear of blood vessels, making them less flexible and more prone to damage, further escalating the risk of cardiovascular issues over time. The body's failure to return to baseline quickly after a stressful event means the cardiovascular system is constantly under strain, with lasting effects on overall heart health. Now imagine doing this every minute, every second of your life.

Think about it—how much stress are we constantly dumping onto our bodies, moment after moment?

Would you call this the art of delayed responses - something we've somehow mastered? Probably not. Whether it's anxiously waiting for a message that feels like it's never going to arrive or struggling to make sense of our feelings long after the moment has passed, these delays might seem frustrating. But ironically, they're also doing a strange kind of magic—quietly shaping our mental and physical well-being in ways we don't even realise.

We've built this glorious system where overclocking our brains, running on constant stress, and drowning in endless delays have become the norm. And the worst part? We don't even seem to care that it's quietly eating away at our mental and physical health—almost as if it's just the "new normal."

Honestly, it's tragic. We barely understand our own brains, our own emotions, even the signals our bodies are desperately trying to send us — yet we keep piling on. More tasks, more information, more delays. And somehow, we expect our minds to just adapt… or perhaps completely short-circuit from the overload!

This reminds me of a thought-provoking conversation I had with a friend recently. They posed an interesting question about the essence of humanity: *If we're inherently wired for survival, shouldn't we, as a species, be even more resilient?*

Perhaps. But what exactly *is* resilience?

Is resilience simply the art of being knocked down over and over, only to be expected to get back up and pretend it didn't hurt? Or is it just positive thinking? Because, honestly, when life hands us lemons, are we really supposed to grin and say, *"Wow, lemons are so refreshing!"*

Oh no, of course not. As someone once told me, resilience is about sitting down and practising mindfulness. That's today's magic bullet—the cure-all, the one-size-fits-all solution, according to the latest self-help gurus and wellness influencers.

Feeling anxious? Meditate! Struggling with work-life balance? Meditate! Want to stop obsessing over that awkward interaction from three years ago? Just sit down, focus on your breath, and—poof!—all of life's little annoyances magically disappear!

Or… perhaps not.

But let's take a closer look…

The Toxic Resilience

We have all heard of the term "mind over matter," which encapsulates the incredible influence the human mind can have over the body and its physical conditions. At its core, the expression suggests that mental strength and willpower can overcome any limitations, ailments, and challenges. This concept is deeply rooted in human philosophy and psychology, emphasising the connection between the mind and body and the potential for the mind to shape reality.

Let's be real for a second. Mindfulness is great, but it's not exactly the Swiss Army knife of solutions we've all been led to believe. While it's easy to get swept up in the mindfulness movement that's all the rage these days, let's not pretend that this ancient practice is going to fix every problem in our hyper-distracted, stress-obsessed, Wi-Fi-addicted world. Here's my take on so-called "resilience", getting way more credit than it actually deserves and why it's certainly not the only solution.

I remember when I was young and often felt tired; my father would say, "At this age, no one feels tired." Although he meant this to encourage and build resilience in me, as a child, I took it literally. I struggled to understand how to find balance, and over time, this belief became ingrained in me. Now, when I feel tired, I question whether I am pushing myself hard enough despite having a better understanding of things as an adult.

This is a classic example of how we inadvertently shape and influence young minds without any ill intentions. We often forget that, until a certain age, a child's mind is not fully developed to process or comprehend many concepts — a crucial aspect I will explore further in relation to technology later in this book.

While mindfulness practices can help with stress management (if you have the time and emotional bandwidth to engage), they're not a quick-solve for the complex, multifaceted mess that is modern life.

Let's face it: If you've been overworked for weeks, dealing with family drama, and then someone suggests you "just breathe," you're more likely to roll your eyes than to suddenly feel enlightened. No amount of deep breathing is going to fix that sinking feeling in your stomach when you realise you've just been ghosted by your boss for the third time this month. Mindfulness can help navigate stress — but it's no magical reset button.

The idea of mind over matter is not a modern invention. Ancient philosophers like Plato and Aristotle mused about the power of the mind to control the body, even suggesting that the soul and mind could transcend the physical world. Buddhist and Hindu traditions have long emphasised the power of meditation and mental discipline to achieve both physical and spiritual transformation. Philosophers such as René Descartes, who famously declared, "Cogito, ergo sum" ("I think, therefore I am"), highlighted the centrality of the mind in human existence.

The placebo effect is another powerful example of mind over matter. It occurs when people experience real improvements in their health after receiving treatment with no active ingredients simply because they believe it will work. The concept of "mental toughness" in sports and organisations - such as visualisation, affirmations, and goal-setting - has enhanced performance by improving focus, determination, and resilience.

The mind certainly has undeniable power. Studies show that the brain can trigger biochemical changes in the body based on belief alone. However, it's important to be able to recognise when our strength starts to become a weakness.

The idea of mind over matter can sometimes be misinterpreted as suggesting that individuals are solely responsible for their struggles, which can lead to feelings of guilt or inadequacy. It's crucial to approach the idea with balance because, like anything, over-resilience, where individuals feel compelled to withstand extreme stress or hardship without addressing or acknowledging their emotional, mental, or physical needs, can turn resilience toxic, leading to persistent self-neglect, emotional suppression, and an unhealthy sense of responsibility to "tough it out". Toxic resilience comes from an innate desire to be strong or brave. It is often exacerbated by external pressures such as cultural or societal. The emphasis on "keep going" or "never give up" leads many to ignore their emotional or physical needs, suppressing feelings of fatigue and stress in favour of pushing forward.

The desire to appear "strong and successful" often leads people to hide their true feelings, shy away from vulnerability, and sometimes distance themselves from friends and family in order to maintain an image of perfection. The fear of judgment or the relentless quest for social validation can compel individuals to push through, even when they are emotionally or physically drained. This forced sense of "resilience" becomes toxic when it leads people to suppress their struggles, fearing they will be seen as weak or incapable.

In Indian society, the idea of resilience is not just ingrained – it's a cultural cornerstone, one that holds enduring hardship in the highest regard, often at the cost of emotional expression or seeking help. This mindset thrives in Indian families, where "grit" is hailed as a virtue and "fighting through adversity" is passed down like a sacred tradition. While this builds strength and determination, it can also stifle emotional well-being, burying unresolved trauma and mental health struggles beneath a façade of toughness. In the relentless culture of "toughing it out," these issues often go unnoticed, quietly festering in the shadows.

Technology today has given rise to the "hustle" mentality, which encourages individuals to continue non-stop in the pursuit of success. Platforms like Instagram, LinkedIn, and TikTok often glorify entrepreneurs, influencers, and workers who constantly strive to learn, grow, and achieve high levels of success. While motivation and ambition can be positive, the constant "hustle culture" fosters an environment where rest and self-care are seen as weaknesses. Social media, while a great tool for knowledge and expression, also amplifies unrealistic expectations. These platforms often showcase the most polished versions of people's lives, usually depicting an idealised image of success, happiness, and productivity. When users see others seemingly thriving, it creates a sense of inadequacy for those who are struggling or facing challenges, creating pressure to portray oneself as resilient, even when things aren't going well.

Another way technology cultivates toxic resilience is through the emphasis on data-driven performance metrics. From fitness trackers to work productivity apps, people are increasingly being measured and quantified in nearly every aspect of their lives. Fitness apps encouraging users to hit certain step counts or exercise targets can sometimes foster a mindset where physical resilience becomes synonymous with exceeding goals, even when the body signs the need for rest. These tools track everything from steps taken to hours worked and offer metrics that suggest what "success" or "resilience" should look like. The relentless pursuit of these metrics can drive people to push themselves beyond their limits, trying to reach arbitrary standards set by algorithms or external expectations, such as comparison against others, which leads to the notion that resilience means achieving more - no matter the cost.

However, one of the most obvious and significant ways technology today is fostering toxic resilience is by promoting an "always-on" culture. Smartphones, laptops, and other connected devices keep us perpetually reachable, available, and on-call - whether for work, social obligations, or digital consumption. The proliferation of technology has blurred the lines between work and personal life, making it harder for individuals to maintain healthy boundaries. With the advent of remote work, mobile apps, and cloud-based services, many people are now expected to be available for work around the clock. The technology-driven culture of being "always on" reinforces the idea that resilience means being constantly productive, without the need for rest, creating a sense of obligation where individuals feel that they must respond to work emails, messages, or deadlines at any time of day or night, pushing themselves further than what is sustainable.

The brevity and convenience of digital communication lead individuals to suppress their true emotions, fearing that expressing vulnerability or asking for help will be seen as a weakness. People avoid discussing personal struggles or mental health issues because they feel that doing so would disrupt the resilient persona they have cultivated. Instead of opening up, people continue pushing themselves to appear strong and unaffected while bottling up their emotions.

This cycle of emotional suppression fosters a sense of isolation—an ironic reality in which we are constantly connected yet increasingly lonely. Astonishingly, the very medium designed to enhance communication amplifies disconnection, as we will explore next.

The Digital Dialogue

Communication is one of the most fundamental aspects of human civilisation, and in many cultural contexts, it holds an especially profound significance. Over millennia, it has evolved in ways that have profoundly shaped societies, enabling the exchange of ideas, collaboration, and the growth of cultures. From the ancient oral traditions of the Vedas to the lightning-fast messages of the digital age, the journey of communication is a testament to humanity's ingenuity, resilience, and relentless pursuit of connection.

The earliest forms of communication can be traced back to prehistoric cave paintings, some of which date as far back as 30,000 years ago, in regions such as the Bhimbetka caves in Madhya Pradesh (MP, India). These visual symbols, often depicting hunting scenes or abstract designs, were used to convey information or record events. While the West was producing iconic cave paintings in Lascaux and Altamira, the Indian subcontinent was also fostering its own form of prehistorical communication. Ancient Indian art and sculpture, such as the stone carvings at the Ajanta and Ellora caves, were not just artistic expressions but a means of preserving and communicating moral, spiritual, and philosophical teachings.

Parallel to visual art, humans developed oral communication. Language, though initially rudimentary, allowed for the sharing of stories, cultural values, and survival techniques. The oral tradition in India is especially rich, from the Vedas and Upanishads to the epics of the Mahabharata and Ramayana, which were transmitted orally for centuries before being written down. These sacred texts formed the cornerstone of early Indian society, preserving knowledge across generations. As much as the Western world embraced written forms of communication, the Indian tradition highly valued oral transmission, symbolised by the presence of oral Gurus and spiritual masters who conveyed wisdom in person.

However, Johannes Gutenberg's invention of the printing press in the 15th century transformed the landscape of communication. By making books and pamphlets accessible to the masses, the printing press democratised knowledge and spurred movements such as the Renaissance and the Reformation. Literacy rates soared, and newspapers began shaping public opinion, heralding the age of mass communication.

The 19th century ushered in the era of broadcast media. Radio and television revolutionised how people consumed information, entertainment, and news. With the rise of modern newspapers, the press became an instrumental tool for social reform and resistance, serving as a medium through which national leaders could communicate their vision to the masses. Radio, television, and later the internet revolutionised the way people consumed information, just as they did worldwide, but they also enabled a uniquely regional perspective on these global platforms. For example, in India, Television started the storytelling tradition with shows such as *Ramayan* and *Mahabharat*, which not only entertained but educated and strengthened cultural identity.

In the late 20th century, the advent of the internet was a watershed moment in the evolution of communication. Initially designed as a tool for researchers, the internet rapidly grew into a global network. Email, the first widely adopted internet communication tool, transformed professional and personal correspondence. India's IT revolution, beginning in the 1990s, played a central role in this global shift. Cities like Bengaluru became known as the "Silicon Valley" of Asia, driving technological advancements that are now pivotal in shaping global digital communication.

That said, it was the 21st century that truly sparked a revolution in communication technologies, fuelled by digital innovation. The rise of smartphones, social media, and apps like WhatsApp and Zoom has seamlessly integrated instant communication into our everyday routines. The convenience of features like video calls, emojis, and AI-driven language translation has not only made interactions more engaging but also vastly improved accessibility. Today, we can't help but marvel at these technological leaps, realising just how far we've come in connecting with each other, anytime, anywhere.

Picture a world with over 8 billion people, all connected instantly!

However, these advancements have also brought about shifts in how we communicate. For instance, face-to-face interactions are increasingly being replaced by text or video chats, which, while convenient, often fall short of capturing the emotional depth and nuance of in-person conversations. The richness of personal connection seems to be fading, as we become more dependent on quick, impersonal digital exchanges.

Scientific studies have shown that a face-to-face interaction is far more effective than digital communication in fostering emotional bonds. Research from the University of California, Los

Angeles (UCLA) has shown that nonverbal cues such as facial expressions and body language significantly contribute to the richness of human interaction. These cues trigger the release of neurochemicals such as oxytocin, which strengthens trust and empathy in relationships. This explains why digital communication, despite its efficiency, can often feel shallow, as it lacks these vital sensory cues. While digital platforms encourage connections among people, they also lead to misunderstandings and conflicts. The anonymity of the internet has contributed to issues like cyberbullying and trolling, which can harm mental health and disrupt societal cohesion. Balancing the benefits and drawbacks of technological communication is an ongoing challenge, one that requires our continued engagement and understanding.

The emotional impact of digital communication becomes even more pronounced when considering the phenomenon of "phubbing" – ignoring people physically present in favour of engaging with one's smartphone. This behaviour, as studies have shown, can lead to a significant increase in feelings of loneliness and depression. The potential negative impact of digital communication on mental health is a significant concern in the current era.

That said, in an age where smartphones are within reach 24/7, social media platforms facilitate instantaneous interactions, and global news travels at the speed of light, it is paradoxical that many people feel lonelier than ever before. The unprecedented level of digital connectivity has, in many ways, created an equally unprecedented sense of emotional isolation. This phenomenon is reshaping how we interact, perceive relationships, and understand the very fabric of human connection.

Research from the *Journal of Social and Clinical Psychology* suggests that overuse of digital media can alter the brain's reward system. In some cultures, one might find solace in practices such as yoga and meditation, both of which have been scientifically shown to reduce stress and improve emotional well-being by enhancing mindfulness and promoting neural integration. However, the overuse of instant messaging and social media seems to fuel a cycle of instant gratification, undermining our capacity for deep, reflective engagement.

If we read any articles about loneliness recently, it is apparent that the Western world, specifically, is facing an epidemic of loneliness. The number of lonely people has exploded over the past several decades, while researchers have found that feeling lonely is as dangerous for our health as smoking 15 cigarettes a day.

The obvious question that comes to our mind is that, despite living in an era of unprecedented technological connectivity, why do so many people experience feelings of loneliness and isolation? Why suicide rates are a growing concern in certain regions and demographics globally? While there are, no doubt, many reasons that have contributed to us feeling lonelier - capitalism, neoliberalism, individualism, globalisation, and changes to communication.

This is why, as part of my dissertation, I wanted to dig deeper into something that has always intrigued me — *why, despite living in the most connected era, so many of us feel lonelier than ever*. This paradox of modern life isn't just frustrating; it has real consequences for mental health.

With digital communication becoming such a huge part of our lives, I wanted to explore a few key questions:

- Do personality traits shape how connected or lonely we feel?

- How do online interactions affect mental health, and does a sense of belonging make a difference?

- Does it matter more who we connect with and why, rather than just how often we interact?

I had over 100 people take part, and the results were eye-opening.

This study challenged the idea that simply interacting more makes us feel closer to others. Instead, it revealed something far more important — **who** we connect with and **why** matters more than **how often** we connect. Social media and online connections can be lifelines for some, but for those without strong family ties, self-awareness, and a deep sense of relatedness, they can make loneliness even worse.

Let's be real: humans are wired for connection. Our powerful brains and advanced intelligence evolved largely because of our need for social interaction. A huge portion of our neocortex is dedicated to social cognition, helping us navigate relationships and understand others. But despite all our technological advancements, the human brain hasn't fully adapted to digital communication — and for good reason. One of the biggest challenges is the absence of nonverbal cues like facial expressions, body language, and tone of voice. These subtle signals provide essential context, and without them, our brains struggle to interpret meaning in a way that aligns with how we naturally process and understand social interactions.

Human conversations trigger a far richer hormonal response than digital ones, thanks to multisensory inputs. These hormones—linked to trust, empathy, and bonding—help strengthen our relationships on a deeper level. While digital communication plays a valuable role in maintaining connections, it fails to satisfy the brain's deeper need for human closeness. That said, technological communication is undeniably convenient, offering a quick and efficient way to stay in touch. But it lacks the depth and multisensory engagement our brains rely on to fully register an interaction. From a psychological and philosophical standpoint, digital communication is merely an illusion of connection—one that our brains struggle to process as truly fulfilling.

The easiest way to understand this is through the analogy of a liquid diet. While a liquid diet can provide essential nutrients and calories, the brain doesn't perceive it as real food. This is because our brains have evolved to process food in a specific way—through sensory feedback like texture, chewing, smell, and even the feeling of stomach stretching as we digest. Our minds associate food with these tactile experiences, making solid meals feel more satisfying. Even though liquid diets can be nutritionally complete, the hormonal and metabolic responses they trigger are different from those caused by solid food.

Online interactions are undoubtedly real in terms of the emotions they can evoke, the communication they enable, and the actions they inspire. However, the depth and quality of these connections vary, combined with the lack of hormonal response and essential sensory context that a human brain requires, making them appear superficial and illusory to a human brain. Oxytocin is typically released during physical touch or in close, personal interactions. Technological communications - such as texting, messaging, and even video calls lack this element.

Technology has changed not just our mode of communication but our communication style too.

In today's fast-paced world, traditional written text often takes too much time and feels inadequate for conveying emotions, humour, and complex ideas.

Today, we want to communicate as quickly and briefly as possible – thanks to our need for instant gratification. Here, we enter the world of Emojis and GIFs, providing a way to convey emotions, reactions, or information instantly, without the need for lengthy explanations or sentences. A single emoji or a quick GIF is often enough to express an idea, feeling, or reaction more swiftly than typing out a detailed message.

These dynamic and visually driven forms of communication have become integral to our digital interactions. These cultural staples are not only reshaping the way we connect but also influencing how our brains process and respond to information.

It's a fact that the brain processes visuals faster than text. Studies show that images are processed up to 60,000 times quicker than written words, and visuals improve comprehension and retention. This makes GIFs and memes highly effective in grabbing attention and evoking emotional responses. Studies have shown that a humorous meme can trigger the release of dopamine, the brain's "feel-good" neurotransmitter, fostering a sense of pleasure.

That said, there are potential downsides. These formats diminish traditional communication skills, such as nuanced verbal articulation or critical reading and writing abilities. Memes and GIFs often reduce nuanced topics into bite-sized, oversimplified messages. As a result, our communication style changes. We constantly look for more simplified interactions and avoid thoughtful and deeper engagement.

Quick visual communication like GIFs can also oversimplify emotions, potentially hampering individuals' ability to recognise and express genuine feelings. Our brains ultimately adapt to the constant exposure to short, punchy content, making it difficult for individuals to focus on longer or more in-depth forms of information.

The preference for quick, visual communication (like emojis, GIFs, or video clips) further dilutes the depth of interpersonal communication. Over-reliance on these mediums leads to superficial relationships. Substituting meaningful conversations with quick visual exchanges weakens the emotional bonds and understanding between individuals.

Most significantly, however, the immediacy of fast communication has encouraged knee-jerk reactions rather than reflective responses. This is especially evident in online arguments or "cancel culture." In recent years, the term "cancel culture" has become a lightning rod in discussions surrounding accountability, free speech, and the dynamics of power in the digital age.

At its core, cancel culture refers to the phenomenon of publicly calling out individuals, companies, or institutions for behaviour or actions deemed offensive, unethical, or unacceptable, often leading to consequences such as boycotts, loss of opportunities, or reputational damage.

Proponents of cancel culture argue that it empowers ordinary people to challenge power structures and demand accountability. In a world where traditional institutions often fail to address systemic injustices, cancel culture has brought attention to issues ranging from workplace harassment to racial discrimination.

Critics, however, caution against the darker side of cancel culture, as it can devolve into a form of public shaming that lacks nuance and denies individuals the opportunity for growth or redemption. The rapid spread of information - and misinformation -on social media can lead to disproportionate responses, punishing individuals without due process.

Additionally, the fear of being "cancelled" can stifle open dialogue and creativity. Scholars and public figures have expressed concerns that cancel culture discourages people from voicing unpopular or controversial opinions, thus undermining the principles of free speech and healthy debate. In some cases, cancel culture has been co-opted by bad actors to silence dissent or target individuals unfairly. The blurred lines between accountability and vengeance make it challenging to assess when cancel culture is being wielded responsibly.

Workplace communication is another domain profoundly affected by technological advancement. Traditional forms of communication, such as face-to-face meetings and phone calls, have been supplemented - or in some cases replaced - by a wide variety of digital tools and platforms. These changes have impacted how we collaborate, share information, and even build relationships at work. One of the most significant impacts of technology on workplace communication is the speed at which we can exchange information. Instant messaging platforms allow employees to communicate in real-time, ask questions, or provide feedback without delays. This has made the workplace faster and more responsive.

With digital tools and data-driven insights, feedback can be tracked, analysed, and quantified, giving people more detailed insights into employee performance. For example, project management tools can show how long tasks take to complete, helping managers provide more targeted feedback. In some organisations, technology has allowed for greater visibility and direct access to leadership.

While technology has brought about significant improvements in workplace communication and efficiency, it has also introduced several challenges that negatively impact workplace relationships and the way we interact with colleagues. Virtual interactions tend to be more task-oriented and less personal, which can reduce the depth of relationships between coworkers. Casual chats in the breakroom or informal hallway conversations are now lost, making relationships more transactional and less relational.

The ease of sending messages via email, chat apps, and project management tools has led to an overload of communication. Effective communication in the workplace relies heavily on emotional intelligence - the ability to recognise and manage one's own emotions, as well as the emotions of others. Technology hinders the development of this skill.

It's ironic that the tools designed to bring us closer have also built invisible walls. The emotional nuance of a conversation—tone, facial expressions, or body language—is lost in translation. The fast-paced communication styles have altered our brains and behaviour today. Lack of empathy, ADHD, aggression and many other mental illnesses are now becoming so common that we do not even see them as illnesses anymore unless they become significantly extreme.

In a world increasingly dominated by technology, our collective patience has become a casualty of convenience. Digital innovations that promise to save time and increase efficiency are, paradoxically, shortening our attention spans and reducing our tolerance for delay.

But it's not the end - the challenges presented by technology are surely complex, but they are not insurmountable. Just as we have adapted to and excelled in technology, we must find ways to preserve our deep-rooted cultural traditions of human connection, empathy, and personal interaction.

The Dopamine Trap

After a long day, travelling back home on the Tube, we often find ourselves reaching for our phones, seeking a quick distraction. Open Facebook! It's a familiar routine, isn't it?

Let's be honest—we all do it. After a long, exhausting day, we feel justified in taking a break, mindlessly scrolling through amusing memes or funny videos, convincing ourselves that it's just a harmless way to unwind. Those colourful ads, curated posts, and bite-sized distractions offer a fleeting sense of happiness, making us feel momentarily lighter.

And just like that, we take our first step into the dopamine trap!

What starts as a simple decision to de-stress quickly turns into a cycle of low-effort engagement, unknowingly activating our brain's reward-seeking behaviour. Each new post, meme, or vacation snapshot triggers a dopamine spike, pulling us deeper into an endless loop of instant gratification. Like addictive substances such as nicotine or cocaine, our brain begins to crave the next hit, making the habit harder to break.

Over time, this sensitisation fuels a compulsive behaviour cycle—where the initial rush fades faster, leaving us chasing that fleeting pleasure with increasing urgency, trapped in a loop that never quite satisfies. Instead of feeling satisfied with what we have or thinking about activities that may reap long-term benefits, we feel content with the immediate reward these posts offer - a feeling disconnected from the daily hustle and bustle.

Such cycles are not new, but they are becoming increasingly prevalent with the ubiquity of smartphones. Scientists have identified a strong correlation between addiction and dopamine desensitisation, which occurs when our brain is overstimulated over prolonged periods. With too much stimulation, fewer dopamine receptors are available to process the chemical, leading to a range of negative consequences — fatigue, sleep disorders, lack of motivation, and procrastination.

It's not about any single post or comment. It's about the anticipation and the regularity with which our brain receives that little rush. Every scroll and every post becomes an opportunity for another hit of dopamine. And it doesn't just stop there. As we continue to scroll, we notice other things. We see people doing something fun, exciting, or rewarding. The constant bombardment of dopamine-releasing stimuli can lead to dopamine desensitisation or dopamine depletion. This means that the brain becomes less responsive to dopamine over time, requiring more stimulation to achieve the same feeling of pleasure or reward. More importantly, in no time, this becomes our second nature.

In recent decades, the world has experienced a profound shift in how we access information and more importantly, how quickly we expect it. From services like Amazon Prime and Uber Eats to streaming platforms like Netflix, we've become accustomed to getting what we want without waiting. It is a cultural shift driven by technologies designed to deliver instant gratification, which in turn appeals to the brain's reward system.

Every instant reply, auto-played video, or one-click purchase results in a dopamine release, reinforcing this behaviour. The ease and speed of modern life certainly have their benefits—convenience and productivity—but they also make us more prone to frustration when we encounter delays or slower-paced situations.

At its core, instant gratification appeals to the brain's reward system. When we receive a text reply, watch a video that auto-plays, or complete an online transaction with a swipe, our brain releases dopamine, reinforcing the behaviour. This process is amplified by technology's deliberate design.

Services like Amazon, Uber, and more exemplify the "instant gratification thrift," where convenience precedes patience. The result is a culture increasingly accustomed to immediate results.

The shift is not inherently negative. The ability to fulfil needs quickly has improved the quality of life in many ways. However, it has also conditioned us to expect instant results in all areas of life, from customer service to personal interactions, creating frustration when reality does not meet these high-speed expectations. Social media platforms are a major driver of this decline in patience. These platforms are designed to deliver quick, dopamine-inducing rewards.

A 2015 study by Microsoft revealed that the average human attention span dropped from 12 seconds in 2000 to just 8 seconds by 2013. This reduction has even been compared to the attention span of a goldfish, which is about 9 seconds. We are speaking and writing faster than before, and we consume news, engage in conversations, and build relationships more superficially as a result.

From a neurological perspective, technology stimulates the brain's reward system, reinforcing behaviours that favour immediacy. Each notification, message, or search result triggers a release of dopamine, creating a feedback loop that prioritises quick rewards over sustained, meaningful efforts. Over time, this rewiring makes it increasingly difficult to delay gratification or focus on tasks requiring prolonged attention.

We may not even notice some of our behavioural changes, but one research has proved that humans today speak and write faster than in the past. It can be examined from several perspectives, including how we consume information, engage in conversations, build relationships, and even how we walk. Shallow interactions often replace deep, meaningful connections, leading to a society prioritising speed over substance.

Over time, this rewiring makes it harder to delay gratification or endure situations requiring sustained attention. The consequences extend beyond our personal lives. In workplaces, employees struggle with tasks requiring focus or become frustrated with slow processes. In education, students accustomed to instant answers find it challenging to engage deeply with complex subjects. This rapid pace has brought benefits such as convenience and productivity, but it also has significant consequences, including increased stress, reduced quality of life, and the erosion of work-life balance. As a result, today, we constantly find ways to slow down and reclaim moments of pause in our fast-paced lives.

The decline in patience has societal ramifications. Road rage, shorter tempers, and reduced tolerance for differing opinions are symptoms of a culture increasingly unwilling to wait or endure discomfort. This trend is evident in political discourse, where quick soundbites often overshadow nuanced debate. Moreover, the environmental impact of this impatience cannot be ignored. The demand for fast fashion, one-day delivery, and disposable goods contributes to unsustainable practices driven by our need for immediacy.

This is why, in the digital age, dopamine - a neurotransmitter known as the "feel-good" chemical - has taken centre stage in discussions about technology's impact on human behaviour.

Dopamine's primary function is to reinforce behaviours that promote survival and pleasure. In a natural setting, this could mean motivating us to eat, reproduce, or achieve social bonds. However, technology has effectively hijacked this system. Social media platforms, for example, are designed to trigger frequent dopamine releases through likes, comments, and notifications. Each time a user receives validation or new information, a small dopamine spike occurs, reinforcing the habit of checking their device and creating a feedback loop of desire and reward. Gaming is another area where dopamine plays a significant role. Video game designers leverage the neurotransmitter by incorporating rewards like achievements, surprise elements, and progression systems. These mechanisms not only engage players but also keep them returning for more, sometimes to the detriment of their mental health and productivity. Similarly, endless scrolling on platforms like Instagram or TikTok exploits the brain's dopamine response to unpredictability, creating an addictive cycle of searching for the next "hit."

This also leads to another psychological disorder: FOMO, or the Fear of Missing Out. People's posts about events, vacations, or accomplishments lead us to a feeling of FOMO, which further strengthens our desire to engage. We start to feel that if we do not do this, we will be left behind. We begin to believe that this is not bad but a way to keep us updated and connected.

In countries like, India, where once family connections, cultural practices, and social bonds have always played a central role in daily life, we are now witnessing the effects of this technological shift. While modernisation brings progress, it also poses a challenge to traditional values of patience, contemplation, and emotional connection. To counteract these changes, we must cultivate mindful practices in our daily routines — family time, outdoor activities, and simple, undistracted conversations. We must teach delayed gratification, especially to younger generations, and emphasise the importance of long-term goals over instant rewards.

A culture obsessed with short-term rewards may struggle to maintain focus on long-term objectives. Studies show that chronic overactivation of dopamine pathways can lead to extreme desensitisation, requiring more intense stimuli to achieve the same level of satisfaction. This can make individuals prone to issues like addiction and grave mental health issues such as anxiety and depression.

This highlights the criticality of comprehending dopamine's role in creating healthier digital habits. In today's ever-connected world, the allure of instant gratification has never been stronger. And again, the solution is not to abandon technology but to use it mindfully.

Practices like prioritising family time, engaging in outdoor activities, encouraging meaningful mealtime conversations, focusing on long-term goals, and teaching delayed gratification from an early age are essential steps in countering the negative effects of technology.

Here, parents play a pivotal role. Children, especially in their formative years, are highly impressionable and often look to their parents for guidance in developing healthy habits. By encouraging outdoor activities and fostering a culture of delayed gratification, parents can help mitigate the risks of technology overuse. Additionally, engaging in meaningful family activities, such as shared meals and board games, can create opportunities for deeper connections and conversations that are less likely to be interrupted by digital distractions. Furthermore, parents can model mindful use of technology themselves, teaching their children the importance of balance and self-control in an increasingly instant-gratification-driven world.

The age of technology offers tremendous opportunities for growth and connection, but it also requires a conscious effort to maintain balance. By recognising the allure of instant gratification and striving for mindful consumption, we can harness the benefits of technology and build a society that values patience, resilience, and meaningful progress.

Mastery, Control, Self-Reliance

Speaking of the dopamine trap—there's another layer to it. The thrill of indulgence doesn't begin with the first bite; it starts long before. Dopamine doesn't wait for me to sink my fork into Tiramisu— it's already working its magic the moment I step into that cosy Italian café, wrapped in the rich aroma of espresso and the promise of indulgence. But here's the thing: it's not really about the dessert. It's the anticipation, the certainty, the delicious sense of knowing exactly what's coming, that sets my brain alight. And that's where control comes in. Because in that moment, I'm not just craving pleasure - I'm craving certainty, predictability, the feeling that I'm in charge of what happens next. But am I really? Or is my brain playing me at my own game?

When we believe we can shape what happens next, our brain treats it like a victory, delivering a rewarding rush of dopamine. It's like a clever mental hack that turns life's unpredictability into something a bit more manageable.

Control is that secret ingredient in every dish of our lives — we crave it, we seek it, and sometimes, we even fight for it. Just look at the world today — wars, conflicts, power struggles — at their core, they all boil down to control. It's hardwired into our psychology, shaping everything from the smallest choices, like deciding what to have for lunch, to the grand ambitions of reshaping societies. Whether we're arranging our surroundings, steering our personal lives, or subtly nudging others in a certain direction, the need for control isn't just a preference — it's woven into the very fabric of what it means to be human.

And then comes the Bhagavad Gita, offering a paradox: *we're entitled to our actions but not their outcomes.* If that's the case, why do we cling so fiercely to control?

Perhaps it's because, even though we know we can't control every outcome, we feel compelled to try. And how we navigate that tension — the constant push and pull between holding on and letting go — doesn't just shape our choices; it shapes our entire experience of life.

In the context of modernity, technology has not only transformed how we express our desire for control but has also amplified it in ways we never imagined. Its role in shaping human behaviour and decision-making cannot be overstated.

From the earliest days of civilisation, tools of control have been fundamental to human progress — fire gave us the power to cook and protect ourselves, the wheel revolutionised transportation and agriculture, and each subsequent invention extended our ability to shape the world around us. Today, modern technology has taken this impulse to new heights, embedding the need for control into every aspect of our personal, social, and professional lives.

With each innovation, we gain new ways to manage, manipulate, and influence our surroundings—both physically and digitally. The more we rely on technology, the more it reinforces this drive, making control not just a tool for survival but an intrinsic part of how we navigate the world.

The advent of smart homes, equipped with IoT devices, allow us to regulate our environments with ease—whether adjusting lighting, temperature, or security. Similarly, weather applications, now so ubiquitous, enable users to predict atmospheric changes and prepare for potential disruptions, further enhancing the illusion of mastery over nature.

Calendars, reminders, and scheduling apps have become indispensable tools in our pursuit of control—over our time and the structure of our lives. By automating repetitive tasks, technology allows us to delegate routine responsibilities to machines, reinforcing our sense of mastery over time. This not only enhances efficiency but also creates the illusion that we are reclaiming control—

freeing up time for more meaningful activities, or at least making us believe we are the ones deciding how to spend it. Yet, ironically, instead of feeling more in control, we only seem to be getting busier!

The internet has revolutionised our ability to control information, granting us access to knowledge. With just a few clicks, we tap into vast reservoirs of data, empowering us to make well-informed decisions in every aspect of life — or so we think!

Search engines and AI-driven systems reinforce this sense of control by curating results and delivering personalised insights, shaping what we see based on our preferences. Yet, here's the paradox — while we believe we are mastering knowledge, it is often knowledge that is mastering us.

The more we seek control over information, the more it subtly controls what we think, what we choose, and ultimately, how we navigate the world.

While technology has certainly made us feel more in control, it often creates a false sense of mastery — one that's both fragile and misleading. Take online dating, for instance. You swipe, message, and choose who to connect with, believing you're in full control of your love life. But behind the scenes, algorithms are quietly steering the wheel, showing you people based on hidden patterns and behavioural cues you don't even realise exist. It's like walking into a crowded room, thinking you're choosing who to talk to, only to discover that someone has been subtly guiding you toward a specific group the entire time.

The same illusion plays out across social media, search engines, and recommendation systems. We feel in charge of what we watch, read, and engage with, but in reality, algorithms are curating our digital reality, reinforcing our beliefs and shaping our decisions — often without us even noticing. This invisible influence creates what's known as a "filter bubble" — a personalised echo chamber where we are fed content that aligns with our existing interests, reinforcing our perspectives while quietly narrowing our worldview. So, I come back to my question: *Are we really in control? Or just comfortably controlled?*

Surveillance technologies—from facial recognition to GPS tracking—give us convenience and efficiency, yet they come at the cost of personal autonomy. We unlock phones with our faces, let apps track our locations for real-time recommendations, and rely on AI assistants to anticipate our needs. It all feels seamless, effortless, under our control. But in reality, we have traded privacy for convenience, often without realising the long-term consequences.

The rise of AI in decision-making further complicates this illusion of control. From job recruitment to medical diagnoses, algorithms are increasingly trusted over human judgment. While AI can enhance efficiency, it also reduces personal independence, making individuals more dependent on automated systems and less confident in their own critical thinking and judgments.

Even in our homes, technology dictates more than we realise—parking our cars, dimming our lights, adjusting the thermostat, what to eat, when to walk, where to go on holiday, when to get up, what to think and even how to think! What was once second nature is now delegated to machines, fostering a silent erosion of basic skills. The more we rely on these conveniences, the less we engage in personal decision-making, reinforcing a culture of technological dependence.

This dependence reshapes our mental and cognitive patterns as well. Instant gratification—ordering groceries with a voice command, receiving recommendations before we even ask—chips away at our ability to tolerate delays.

Reminds me of an interesting story. I have a habit of narrating and storytelling—I like to paint the picture, set the scene. But once, tired of my long-winded storytelling, someone said, *"With me, you don't need all the flowery details. You can be direct."*

This is the world we live in now. When they reacted to my words, they weren't really critiquing me—

they were revealing something about themselves. And that's exactly what's happening everywhere — not just in conversations, but in offices, homes, and daily interactions.

We're losing patience! Our ability to sit with complexity, to let a thought unfold, to process information deeply instead of just consuming it quickly — it's all fading!

Somehow, we don't even realise we've trapped ourselves in a vicious cycle — one we created but can't seem to break. The faster we consume, the more impatient we become. And the more impatient we become, the less we let things unfold naturally. We rush everything, squeezing life into bite-sized, instant, no-time-to-waste exchanges.

This impacts everything, from delayed gratification to emotional regulation. Depth is sacrificed for speed, contemplation for convenience, and before we even realise it, our minds are wired for quick hits of information rather than meaningful engagement. And prolonged screen time only accelerates this shift, subtly reshaping our brains in ways we don't yet fully understand — especially during key developmental years, when the foundations of attention, patience, and deep thinking are still being laid.

What began as tools designed to enhance control have, in many ways, ended up controlling us — shaping our decisions, behaviours, and even our fundamental cognitive abilities. The trade-offs between convenience and autonomy are no longer just philosophical concerns; they are deeply embedded in how we function as individuals and as a society

Like control, self-reliance has also become a prized ideal in today's world.

In an era where individualism is celebrated and independence is seen as a virtue, we are taught from a young age that standing on our own two feet is the ultimate goal — whether it's solving our own problems, making our own decisions, or carving out our own path. We pride ourselves on being self-sufficient, believing that true success comes from needing no one but ourselves.

Yet, in a world increasingly shaped by technology, are we truly independent? Or *have we simply shifted our dependence — relying not on people, but on algorithms, automation, and AI to guide our choices, answer our questions, and even think on our behalf?*

Self-reliance, no doubt, is a cornerstone of personal and professional growth. It empowers us to navigate challenges, solve problems, and achieve our goals independently. At its best, it builds confidence, fosters resilience, and gives us a deep sense of accomplishment.

But like any virtue taken to an extreme, over self-reliance can backfire. Too much of it can lead to isolation, burnout, and missed opportunities — something that seems to be happening in today's tech-heavy world.

Technology, which was supposed to enhance self-reliance, has instead created a new kind of dependence. While we claim to be more independent than ever, we rely on AI, algorithms, and digital assistants to make decisions, answer questions, and even handle basic tasks — leaving us less self-sufficient than ever before.

Think about it — when was the last time you asked a person for directions instead of Google Maps? Or relied on your memory instead of a digital note? People turn to Google, Siri, or ChatGPT instead of each other, not just because it's convenient, but because it's easier. No awkward conversations, no fear of judgment, no risk of looking uninformed. With AI, there's no embarrassment, no hesitation — it's always there, always responsive, always ready with an answer.

Yet, the irony is undeniable. The more we turn to technology to be *self-reliant*, the more we lose the very independence we think we're gaining. Instead of figuring things out on our own, we default to quick digital solutions. Instead of developing critical thinking and problem-solving skills, we let algorithms decide for us. Instead of engaging in real conversations, we ask machines to fill the gaps.

In the end, we're not becoming more self-reliant —
we're just outsourcing it!

The internet and technology provide endless access
to information, making it easier than ever to find
solutions to almost any problem. However, this
abundance of information can also be
overwhelming, leading to decision fatigue. With so
many conflicting opinions and resources available,
people may feel pressured to make informed
choices on their own — yet, instead of clarity, they
are often left paralysed by uncertainty.

The proliferation of self-help books, podcasts, and
online courses has created a culture where
individuals feel compelled to fix all their problems
on their own. This constant drive for self-
improvement, fuelled by digital content and social
media, often ignores the reality that not all
problems can be solved independently. The
pressure to achieve success without relying on
others can create unrealistic expectations, leading
to feelings of inadequacy and frustration when
things don't go as planned.

It's important to recognise that many technologies only create an illusion of self-sufficiency. Fitness apps, platforms, and algorithms give users a sense of control, but that's all it is — a sense, an illusion — not true self-reliance.

True self-reliance isn't about doing everything alone — it's about knowing when to lean on others.

Technology has given us incredible tools to solve problems, access resources, and perform tasks independently, but often at a cost. When we replace meaningful interactions with digital shortcuts, we risk losing something far greater than independence — we risk losing what makes us human: collaboration, shared experiences, and emotional connection.

True well-being isn't about distancing ourselves from technology; it's about striking the right balance between self-reliance and meaningful interdependence. The goal isn't to reject technology but to use it intentionally — as a tool, not a replacement for real relationships.

As the saying goes, "Technology is a tool, not a crutch." Strength doesn't come from doing everything alone—it comes from using technology wisely while still nurturing the relationships, communities, and support systems that truly sustain us.

Because in the end, "The greatest wealth is health"—not just physical health, but mental, emotional, and social well-being. And that kind of balance? It doesn't come from an algorithm. It comes from us!

From Print to Pixel

The way humans consume information has undergone a seismic shift over the past few decades. Whether driven by the convenience of not carrying books or the rise of digital devices, the traditional act of reading has been largely replaced or supplemented by screen-based consumption. This transition has sparked ongoing debates about its impact on the brain.

Are devices making us more distracted and less capable of deep thinking? Are books inherently better for fostering comprehension and empathy? To address these questions, we need to explore how the brain processes information differently when interacting with devices compared to books, considering areas such as attention, memory, comprehension, and critical thinking. The intersection of neuropsychology and technology has emerged as a pivotal area of research, examining how different forms of media influence the brain and behaviour.

Whether conscious of it or not, we're constantly being affected by aesthetics – the colour of the walls, the lighting, or the soundscape of the room we're sitting in. Having an aesthetic mindset simply means that we have an awareness of this relationship and are ready to take advantage of it.

As humans, we're constantly processing our surroundings through our senses. What we see, what we hear, what we smell, the temperature and texture of the things we touch. These are the aesthetics of our surroundings, and they're being taken in and processed moment by moment. All of it has the potential to change how we feel. Smells, sounds, and colours can cause our blood pressure to increase or decrease. They can prompt the release of stress hormones or make us feel calm, secure, and sleepy. Most of this is happening on a subconscious level.

Neuroscience tells us that only 5% of our mental activity is conscious. The rest is happening without us even thinking about it. Our senses are being processed, and our emotions are occurring subconsciously. But by increasing our awareness or our aesthetic mindset, we can take all of this into account and begin using art to make lasting changes to our lives and well-being.

One of the most significant differences between consuming content on devices versus traditional methods, such as books or art, lies in how they engage our attention.

Devices – especially smartphones and tablets – are designed to grab attention through multimedia. Each visual cue prompts the brain to shift focus, activating the brain's salience network, which is responsible for detecting novel stimuli. While this adaptability has advantages in fast-paced environments, it comes at the cost of sustained attention. Studies have shown that this can lead to a phenomenon called "continuous partial attention," where individuals are constantly dividing their focus rather than concentrating fully on a single task.

Traditional media sources, such as books, on the other hand, encourage sustained attention. Reading a physical book typically lacks the interruptions inherent to digital media. This enables readers to enter a state of "deep reading," a cognitive process that involves active engagement with the text, sustained focus, and a mental dialogue with the author's ideas. Deep reading activates the default mode network (DMN) of the brain, which is associated with introspection, empathy, and comprehension. Unlike devices, books rarely push readers toward multitasking, allowing the brain to fully process and retain information.

Think about it: We can effortlessly listen to an audiobook while walking, cooking, or juggling a million other things. But the moment we pick up a physical book, everything else comes to a halt. Reading demands our full attention—it refuses to be a background task.

Devices learning often promotes shallow processing due to the nature of digital interfaces, which are designed for quick consumption rather than prolonged engagement. Research indicates that screen readers often skim through text, picking out keywords or phrases rather than deeply engaging with the material. Over time, this habit weakens the brain's ability to build robust memory traces.

Books, on the other hand, pull us into deeper cognitive processing. The simple act of holding a book and flipping its pages creates spatial and contextual cues—think back to what I mentioned earlier about how our minds are wired to respond to sensory input. This tactile experience helps our memory. When we try to recall something from a book, we often visualise its place on the page or remember the sensation of reading a particular chapter. This is what we call the "book memory effect," and it gives us a much stronger cognitive anchor to recall details.

Reading comprehension also differs significantly between devices and books. Digital reading often leads to what researchers call "cognitive offloading," where users rely on the device to store and retrieve information rather than deeply understanding it. The mere presence of hyperlinks can reduce comprehension because the brain must constantly decide whether to click, which disrupts the narrative flow. This multitasking environment makes it harder to form coherent mental models of the text, reducing critical thinking and inferential reasoning.

Books foster a different cognitive experience. When reading a book, especially complex or narrative-driven texts, readers are more likely to engage in inferential thinking and connect ideas across chapters. This process of constructing meaning requires sustained effort and imaginative engagement, both of which are undermined by the digital environment's fast-paced design. Moreover, the physicality of books, combined with their single-purpose nature, enhances comprehension by allowing the brain to fully immerse itself in the text.

Another crucial area where books and devices differ is in fostering empathy and emotional engagement. Studies suggest that reading fiction, in particular, can enhance a reader's ability to understand and empathise with others by simulating real-world social experiences. This is because books often require readers to imagine the thoughts, emotions, and perspectives of characters, a process that activates the brain's theory of mind — a network of regions responsible for understanding others' mental states.

In contrast, digital media, while capable of conveying stories, often dilutes emotional engagement through its fragmented and fast-paced nature. Scrolling through headlines, videos, or social media posts provides less time for reflection and emotional connection. This is also true for audiobooks. Reading a physical book requires more cognitive effort than listening to an audiobook. When we read, we actively decode words and engage with the material, which activates multiple regions of the brain, including those involved in comprehension, memory, and critical thinking.

The brain's plasticity – the ability to adapt and rewire itself based on experiences – means that prolonged use of devices or books can shape neural pathways in distinct ways. Over-reliance on devices can lead to the reinforcement of neural circuits associated with rapid task-switching and superficial scanning, potentially at the expense of circuits involved in deep focus and reflective thinking. Conversely, regular reading of books or spending fun time with family strengthens the neural networks required for sustained attention, deep comprehension, empathy, and critical analysis.

While devices have become indispensable for their convenience, their long-term effects on the brain's cognitive architecture are raising growing concerns.

Researchers warn that constant exposure to fragmented digital content may gradually erode our ability to concentrate deeply and think critically. As our attention becomes more divided, so does our capacity for sustained focus and meaningful learning.

A striking example of this shift occurred in 2009 when Sweden fully embraced technology, replacing traditional textbooks with computers and digital tools. However, fast forward fifteen years, and the country had to rethink its approach. Recognising the cognitive and educational benefits of traditional learning, Sweden is investing 104 million euros to reintroduce books into classrooms between 2022 and 2025 — acknowledging that while technology has its place, it cannot fully replace the depth, engagement, and cognitive benefits that physical books provide.

That said, despite the stark contrast between traditional learning methods and digital tools, it's crucial to recognise that neither devices nor books are inherently "good" or "bad." Each serves a unique purpose, and their impact on the brain largely depends on how they are utilised. Devices offer quick access to information, support multimedia learning, and enable global connectivity. On the other hand, traditional methods continue to excel in fostering deep thought, improving memory retention, and nurturing empathy.

This is why, a balanced approach is ideal for optimising cognitive benefits. Incorporating regular book reading into daily routines can counteract some of the negative effects of digital overexposure. At the same time, mindful use of devices - such as limiting multitasking - can enhance their effectiveness as learning tools. Ultimately, understanding the brain's responses to these mediums empowers us to make informed choices about how we consume information. The link between dopamine, instant gratification, and the need for control is intricate and plays a significant role in shaping behaviours and emotional responses in our modern world.

The need for instant gratification, driven by the brain's dopamine system, intersects with the desire for control, which is amplified by the predictability of rewards in the digital world. While this can feel rewarding in the short term, it can erode long-term satisfaction, making it harder to engage in meaningful, delayed rewards and diminishing our ability to tolerate uncertainty.

Trust & Technology

Not long ago, a handshake sealed a deal, a conversation revealed sincerity, and a word carried real weight. Trust wasn't built on algorithms but on humanity. Today, it's slipping away — not because people have changed, but because technology has redefined how we believe and how our brains process information.

Take communication, for instance. A read receipt with no reply? Suspicious. A delayed response? Worrying. A full day of silence? Basically a crisis. And if someone asks for reassurance or shares their concern? They risk being called needy, dramatic, or just too emotional.

But think about it — did letters ever carry tone? Did a telegram come with context or body language? No. And yet, people trusted the words they received. Back then, no news was assumed to be good news. We didn't just read letters; we tried to understand the unwritten and unspoken without questioning the intent. A clear sign of how technology and societal shifts have rewired our brains to crave speed over depth.

These days, our minds are trapped in surface-level communication—quick, effortless, and shallow. We tell ourselves this is the need of the hour, but it isn't. It's just how our brains think now. We're not really listening; we're just decoding, skimming for meaning without digging deeper. That's why we analyse silences instead of recognising pauses, pick apart delays instead of understanding the weight of time, and second-guess intentions instead of uncovering the real concerns. And in this, we're forgetting how to trust.

It distorts our understanding of connection, making us question sincerity, overanalyse interactions, and even doubt our own feelings. We become hyper-aware of responses—or the lack of them. In the process, we lose sight of what truly matters: genuine presence and patience.

To illustrate, take Regina, a 37-year-old professional from Hungary. She has been using Facebook and Instagram for over a decade, expanding her social circle online by connecting with friends, colleagues, and acquaintances from various stages of her life. Yet, over time, she noticed something strange. She received notifications whenever certain individuals posted updates or shared photos, but others—people she regularly interacted with—seemed to have 'disappeared' from her feed, even though she hadn't unfollowed them.

Sound familiar? Regina's experience is one many of us can relate to. Social media isn't just a platform— it's a carefully curated feed, shaped by algorithms that decide what we see based on what we've engaged with before. The result? Some people and brands dominate our screens, while others fade into the background, buried by the system. What we think is *choice* is really just a digital echo chamber, reinforcing what we already know and like.

In Regina's case, the algorithm began favouring posts from individuals who interacted with her most frequently—friends who liked and commented on her photos, family members who regularly engaged with her status updates, and people with whom she often communicated in group chats. On the other hand, friends with whom she hadn't communicated as often received less visibility.

Now, Regina is an incredibly well-informed person, so this didn't really affect her (Sorry, my friend!). But think about it—this algorithmic adjustment can, and often does, give people the impression that their friends are ignoring them. Even those who know how these algorithms work can't help but feel it. The lack of likes, comments, or even just visibility can start to feel personal.

It happened to me once. I wrote a LinkedIn article, put my heart into it, hit publish... and then— silence. No engagement. And for a moment, I genuinely thought, *Did people not like it?* That's such a human reaction, instinctive even. Let's be real: Social validation, is normal. It takes a conscious effort to step back and remind ourselves that it's not personal, it's just the algorithm doing its thing.

So, going back to my friend, Regina – She, too, began to wonder if certain friends had purposefully distanced themselves or simply lost interest in maintaining their friendship. In reality, the algorithm had just pushed their content out of sight, leaving her feeling isolated and second-guessing the authenticity of her relationships.

On the flip side, Regina received an overwhelming amount of attention from others, whose content was consistently pushed to the top of her feed. These interactions, however, were largely superficial, driven more by likes and comments than by meaningful engagement.

This serves as a clear example of how technology distorts our understanding of what is real, genuine, and authentic.

Trust is a foundational aspect of human society, critical in how individuals and communities interact, build relationships, and navigate the complexities of the world. It enables cooperation, resource-sharing, and functioning within broader systems of norms and expectations. However, in the age of rapid technological advancement, the dynamics of trust are shifting. Technology is not only altering how we build trust with one another but also how we place faith in systems, algorithms, and digital entities.

Historically, trust was grounded in face-to-face interactions and personal experiences. People relied on direct observations, emotional connections, and social cues to determine whether they could trust others. As societies grew larger and more complex, trust extended beyond local networks. It became necessary to place trust in institutions, governments, and organisations — entities with which individuals often had limited personal interaction. This broader societal trust evolved into structural trust, where institutions gained legitimacy based on their role in maintaining order and ensuring fairness.

In the digital age, this structure of trust is being challenged. The question of whom or what to trust—and how and why—has become more complex than ever.

We no longer rely solely on our humanity or the natural abilities of our brains—because, as we saw at the start of this chapter, our brains have already been rewired. And here's the unsettling part: we now live in a world where we can't even fully trust our own rewired minds. The lines between real and reel blur so seamlessly that our perception isn't just influenced—it's shaped, nudged, and subtly distorted.

Once, it was poetic to say that the world we experience is a vivid hallucination. But today? It's becoming a harsh reality.

This is why it's more important than ever to cultivate self-awareness—to recognise how our minds are being shaped and to bring balance, protecting our already rewired brains from being rewired even further.

New devices, emerging technologies, and Artificial Intelligence (AI) solutions are rapidly becoming the backbone of decision-making across industries—finance, healthcare, education, transportation, and beyond. As these systems evolve and grow more autonomous, they are increasingly entrusted with high-stakes decisions that directly impact people's lives.

But with this growing reliance on technology comes a crucial dilemma: *How much is too much? And at what point do we pause to re-evaluate before we lose the human touch?*

Decisions like selecting a life partner, approving loans, or diagnosing life-threatening diseases—once deeply human—are now being handed over to algorithms. Are we really ready for that?

Most people are aware of the *black box* nature of many AI systems—models that operate in ways hidden from the user, offering little to no transparency in how decisions are made. But without transparency, *how* do we trust technology? And more importantly, *for what* can we trust it in real-world situations that directly impact our lives?

Trust hinges on transparency — on the ability to explain the reasoning behind its decisions and, most importantly, its accountability. Yet, in the race to be the first, many of us are failing to pay attention to these crucial safeguards. If technology is to play a larger role in critical sectors, ethical considerations and proper guardrails must remain at the forefront. Only then can we place *meaningful* trust in the technologies shaping our future.

And yet, no matter how advanced technology gets, one thing never changes — the human mind, when it's truly at its best, is still the most powerful, unpredictable, and downright awe-inspiring force out there. And if you need proof, let me take you back to a story most of us know — the story of January 15, 2009.

US Airways Flight 1549 took off from LaGuardia, and just three minutes into the flight, disaster struck: a flock of geese struck both engines, plunging the plane into sudden silence. The computer models suggested it might be possible to return to the airport. Yet, Captain Chesley "Sully" Sullenberger — an experienced pilot who had flown countless flights and faced emergencies before — did not rely solely on simulations. He trusted his human instincts. He made a split-second decision to aim for the Hudson River. Against all odds, he made it happen. Every passenger survived.

This was not just about landing a plane; it was about human experience, intuition, and judgment — qualities that cannot be programmed into an algorithm.

What Sully demonstrated that day was more than extraordinary; it was quintessentially human. It involved courage, wisdom, and an intrinsic understanding of what mattered most in that moment. Ultimately, it wasn't technology that saved those lives; it was a human being who knew exactly what to do when there was no time for second-guessing. As many have said, it was a Miracle on the Hudson.

This story, once again, underscores the value of human capabilities over technology and reaffirms the belief that trust in human instincts remains paramount. While technology has certainly reshaped the landscape of trust, providing opportunities and new possibilities, it is ultimately trust in human judgement that is most essential.

Technology can process vast amounts of data, run simulations, and predict outcomes. However, it is the unique human capacity for judgment that plays an essential role in critical decision-making.

Some experts suggest we might see AI achieve human-level reasoning by 2050, but even then, matching Sully's ability to read a crisis and make life-or-death decisions in real-time remains a significant challenge.

As automation and AI continue to take on greater roles in daily life, they cannot fully replace the human qualities of empathy, judgment, and understanding that underpin authentic trust.

"Manasa, Vacha, Karmana" (By thought, speech, and action) – A reminder from ancient Indian philosophy that trust must be grounded in the alignment of our intentions, words, and deeds. It is imperative that we place our highest degree of trust in human instincts and preserve the human element in decision-making, rather than over-relying on our devices, algorithms or robots.

Shaping Change: Tech's Dual Role

Technology has always fascinated me, which is why I chose this field of work. It's shaped everything around us. Yet not all technological advancements are the same. Some slip seamlessly into our lives, improving what already exists without much disruption. Others arrive like a storm, forcing us to adapt whether we're ready or not.

That's why I think it's important we understand the difference between "technology for change" and "technology of change." Some innovations fix what's broken, making life easier; others completely redefine the world around us, creating new systems and making old ones obsolete.

If we don't recognise this distinction, we risk blindly accepting every new technology without questioning its consequences—or worse, failing to embrace innovations that could genuinely improve our lives. More than ever, I believe we need to think critically about the technology shaping our world so that it serves us, rather than the other way around. So, let's break it down.

Technology for Change

There's a certain kind of technology that works quietly in the background, making things smoother, faster, and more efficient. It doesn't force us to rethink how society functions—it simply helps us progress in ways that feel natural and improves what exists.

We see it everywhere. These are the kinds of technologies that, when introduced, make sense instantly. They solve real problems and makes life more efficient. Technology for Change works within existing systems to make them better, faster, and smarter. It's designed to fix what's broken rather than replace everything we know.

Some examples that stand out:

- Renewable Energy Solutions – Solar panels, wind turbines, and energy-efficient appliances help us reduce our carbon footprint while still using familiar energy systems.

- AI in Healthcare – Predictive algorithms now detect diseases earlier, helping doctors make better decisions and save lives.

- E-Learning Platforms – Apps like Khan Academy and Coursera break down barriers to education, making knowledge accessible to millions.

This type of innovation is all about practicality, precision, and solving real-world problems in a way that feels natural rather than disruptive. It's not the kind that makes headlines for turning industries upside down overnight. Instead, it works quietly in the background, refining and enhancing what already exists, making things smoother, more efficient, and just a little bit better with each step.

What I find most interesting about technology for change is that it rarely meets resistance. Who would complain about better healthcare, smarter farming, or cleaner energy? No one, because these innovations just make life better without turning it upside down.

This is the kind of technology that makes me feel optimistic about progress—it's designed to make life easier, solve real problems, and enhance human potential without breaking everything in the process.

But then, there's the other kind of technology—the one that doesn't just help us move forward but forces us to rethink everything we know. This is where things get tricky because these innovations don't just improve life—they fundamentally alter the way we function as individuals and as a society.

Technology of Change

They disrupt. They don't work within an existing system; they create entirely new ones, often making old ways of doing things obsolete. This is what I call Technology of Change.

Unlike technology for change, which brings steady improvements, this kind upends industries, challenges societal norms, and forces us to adapt. It often comes with excitement and opportunity — but also fear and resistance.

These technologies don't just help us move forward — they force us to change the way we live, work, and think.

A few examples that have completely changed our world:

- The Internet – We went from writing letters to instant messaging, from bookstores to Kindle, from watching the news on TV to endless scrolling on social media. The way we connect, work, and even think has completely changed.

- Blockchain & Cryptocurrencies – Suddenly, we're questioning what money even is and whether banks are necessary. That's a massive shift.

- The Industrial Revolution – Machines didn't just help people work faster; they changed how labour worked entirely, forcing societies to rethink jobs, wages, and economies.

- Smartphones & Social Media – We no longer "go online" – we're always connected. And that has redefined relationships, attention spans, and even self-worth.

These two forces shape how we experience innovation, how industries evolve, and how we adapt as individuals. While they often overlap, their impact on society is vastly different.

The primary distinction lies in intent. Technology for change is solution-oriented, developed to tackle or improve existing systems. It operates within established frameworks to enhance efficiency, accessibility, or inclusivity. For example, the development of prosthetics for disabled individuals or the implementation of electric vehicles (EVs) to reduce carbon footprints are emblematic of this category.

Conversely, the technology of change disrupts or replaces existing paradigms, often rendering previous systems obsolete. It is less about solving a problem within a given framework and more about redefining the framework itself. For instance, the smartphone not only enhanced communication but also created entirely new ecosystems for business, entertainment, and social interaction.

This interplay highlights the dynamic nature of technological evolution, where innovations can evolve from one paradigm to another based-on scale, adoption, and impact. Technology for change and technology of change represent two critical approaches to innovation, each with its unique purpose, impact, and challenges. Understanding and leveraging both paradigms is essential for ensuring that technological advancements are both purposeful and sustainable.

Some of these shifts are necessary. We need change to progress, to solve new challenges, and to keep up with an evolving world. But when a technology is powerful enough to reshape industries, economies, and even the way we think, it demands careful implementation, ethical considerations, and a deep understanding of its long-term consequences.

As we navigate the complexities of the 21st century, the interplay between these paradigms will continue to shape the way we live, work, and think. Whether technology enhances our world or disrupts it entirely, one thing is clear—it must be guided with intent, responsibility, and foresight.

Policymakers, innovators, and society at large must work together to harness the best of both worlds, ensuring that technology serves as a force for progress, equity, and empowerment, rather than an unchecked force that deepens divides or diminishes our humanity. As an ancient Indian saying reminds us, "The light of wisdom will illuminate the path ahead," underscoring the crucial role of knowledge, ethics, and collective action in shaping our future.

As we look ahead, there is one undeniable reality that demands our immediate attention: our planet is changing. Both Technology for Change and Technology of Change will play a defining role in shaping our environmental future. Will these advancements be our greatest ally in restoring balance, or will unchecked progress accelerate the very crisis we seek to solve? We will see in the next chapter.

Unsung Hero of Climate Change

Let's take a moment to praise technology for its ever-growing contribution to the environment. Sure, we might be churning out gadgets, apps, and devices at an unsustainable pace, but have you seen the green tech sector? That's definitely saving the planet, right? Well, clearly, I am being overly sarcastic here! But climate change is real, and there is an urgent need for all of us to be conscious of how our changing behaviour and technology are making things better or worse. *"Jaisi karni, waisi bharni"* (As you sow, so shall you reap) is an apt reminder here, as the consequences of our actions are directly tied to the choices we make today

Technology is often hailed as the saviour of the modern world, capable of transforming industries and solving global challenges. Climate change, however, presents a particularly formidable challenge—one that has also escalated due to technological advancements. While technology can help mitigate the impacts of climate change, it also plays a significant role in driving it. In this chapter, I explore the dual nature of technology's influence on climate change through real-life examples, showcasing both its promise and pitfalls.

One of the most significant ways technology is helping the fight against climate change is through the development and deployment of renewable energy sources. Solar, wind, and hydropower technologies have grown tremendously over the last few decades, providing cleaner alternatives to fossil fuels. Solar energy has seen exponential growth due to advances in photovoltaic (PV) cell technology. In 2023, global solar capacity reached over 1,000 gigawatts, and it's expected to keep growing as costs continue to fall. For instance, China's rapid investment in solar technology has made it the world leader in solar energy production, reducing the need for coal-fired power plants and contributing to global decarbonisation efforts

Electric vehicles, once a niche market, are now becoming mainstream, and this shift could have significant implications for reducing greenhouse gas emissions from the transportation sector.

According to a research, electric vehicles (EVs) have the potential to reduce CO_2 emissions by over 60% compared to gasoline-powered vehicles, depending on the carbon intensity of the energy grid. This highlights the importance of adopting EVs, as the transportation sector accounts for nearly 15% of global greenhouse gas emissions. However, the success of EV adoption also depends on other key factors, such as the development of supporting infrastructure.

Another technological innovation showing promise in the fight against climate change is carbon capture and storage (CCS). CCS technology captures CO_2 emissions from industrial processes and stores them underground, preventing them from entering the atmosphere. The Petra Nova project in Texas, one of the world's largest CCS projects, captures 1.6 million tons of CO2 annually from a coal-fired power plant. The captured CO2 is then stored in deep geological formations, keeping it out of the atmosphere. While still in the early stages of scaling, CCS technology has the potential to play a vital role in meeting global climate targets, particularly for industries that are difficult to decarbonise, such as cement and steel production.

The role of technology in climate change is complex. On one hand, it has provided us with solutions and innovations that have the potential to mitigate the damage caused by our own industrial activities. Renewable energy technologies, electric vehicles, and carbon capture are prime examples of how we can use technology to fight climate change. On the other hand, technology has also fuelled the very problems we face, from fossil fuel dependence and industrial agriculture to the proliferation of e-waste and the environmental cost of data centres.

The mass production of automobiles powered by gasoline and diesel, which began in the early 20th century, revolutionised transportation but also ushered in an era of rising greenhouse gas emissions. Even today, despite the rise of electric vehicles, gas-powered vehicles are still the dominant mode of transportation worldwide, with over 1.4 billion cars on the road. The emissions from these vehicles, combined with oil extraction and refining processes, continue to contribute heavily to global warming.

The use of chemical fertilisers and industrial-scale farming technologies has led to soil degradation, water contamination, and the release of nitrous oxide — a potent greenhouse gas. The expansion of agricultural land has also contributed to deforestation, particularly in tropical regions like the Amazon, where clear-cutting forests for agricultural use has significantly reduced the Earth's capacity to absorb CO_2.

This is still acceptable, but I get anxious when I look at the "ugly" side of technology's role in climate change. It becomes clear that unchecked progress without consideration for the long-term environmental consequences can have catastrophic effects. An example is how Geoengineering technologies are being explored to mitigate the effects of climate change by altering Earth's natural systems. However, the potential consequences of these technologies are largely unknown and could create even greater environmental problems. Solar radiation management (SRM) involves reflecting sunlight away from the Earth to reduce global warming. However, experts warn that SRM could have unpredictable impacts on global weather patterns, including changes in precipitation that could devastate agricultural systems. Additionally, geoengineering technologies might provide a false sense of security, reducing the urgency of addressing the root causes of climate change.

The very technology designed to help combat climate change—such as AI, cloud computing, and machine learning—often contributes significantly to the problem due to its energy consumption. For example, Data centres, which power much of the digital economy, are responsible for around 1% of global electricity use. These centres require massive amounts of energy for cooling and processing data, much of which is still generated from non-renewable sources. As the demand for data and digital services continues to rise, the energy consumption of data centres is expected to increase dramatically, further exacerbating the climate crisis.

Human activities, particularly the burning of fossil fuels, have increased the concentration of greenhouse gases in the atmosphere, leading to significant shifts in weather patterns, sea levels, and ecosystems.

The scientific consensus on climate change is clear: anthropogenic activities, driven largely by technological advancements in industrialisation, energy production, and agriculture, have led to an unprecedented increase in global temperatures. The Intergovernmental Panel on Climate Change (IPCC) has documented a rise of approximately 1.1°C in global temperatures since the preindustrial era, with catastrophic consequences for natural and human systems.

Perhaps a bit of relief comes from the fact that technology, though often blamed for driving climate change, also holds the potential to reverse some of the damage. With the development of cleaner, more efficient systems and solutions, there is hope for a positive shift. The key, however, will be to balance the benefits of technological progress with the necessity for sustainable, climate-conscious decisions and development.

As the saying goes, *"Sabr ka phal meetha hota hai"* — the fruit of patience is sweet. This timeless wisdom reminds us that even though the journey may be long and challenging, the rewards will come if we stay committed with the right intentions and persistence. And nowhere is this lesson more relevant than in the fight against climate change and our growing dependence on technology.

The transition to a greener, more balanced world will not happen overnight. Healing the environment, reducing carbon footprints, and embracing sustainable practices require long-term effort and conscious change.

Technology has made our lives easier, but it has also deepened our environmental footprint—from e-waste to energy-intensive data centres, from resource-hungry gadgets to a culture of disposability. Every new phone, laptop, or smart device carries a hidden environmental cost, from mining rare earth metals to excessive power consumption. So, while innovation plays a role in tackling climate change, we must not fall into the trap of technological overdependence

Smart Health

In the world today, healthcare and technology are having the most thrilling, boundary-pushing, awe-inspiring romance of all time. If you thought a simple visit to the doctor was about real human connection, you've clearly been living under a rock. The future of healthcare is a flashy digital interface, an algorithm, and a robot telling you, "Your symptoms are... inconclusive. Please consult your app."

What once seemed like a distant dream - accessible, efficient, and personalised healthcare - is now becoming a reality. The fusion of advanced technologies with medical care is reshaping how we prevent, diagnose, treat, and manage diseases, offering more promise than ever before. But as with any innovation, there are both immense benefits and challenges that come with it.

In recent years, the integration of technology in healthcare has revolutionised the way medical services are delivered, accessed, and managed. From diagnostic tools powered by artificial intelligence (AI) to telemedicine platforms that connect patients to providers virtually, the synergy between technology and healthcare is reshaping the industry. This transformation holds immense promise for improving patient outcomes, reducing costs, and addressing global healthcare disparities.

Advancements in AI and machine learning have empowered healthcare professionals to detect diseases with unprecedented accuracy. Tools like AI-powered imaging systems can analyse X-rays, CT scans, and MRIs to identify abnormalities, often with greater precision than human radiologists. For instance, AI has shown remarkable success in detecting early signs of cancers, such as breast or lung cancer, enabling timely interventions.

Wearable devices, like smartwatches, fitness trackers, and specialised health gadgets, are reshaping how we monitor and manage our health.

These devices track everything from heart rate, sleep patterns, and calories burned to more advanced metrics such as blood oxygen levels, ECG readings, and even blood glucose levels.

For people with chronic conditions like diabetes, wearables have become essential in managing their health on a day-to-day basis. Smartwatches, for instance, can alert users when their heart rate becomes irregular or when blood oxygen levels drop below normal, providing early warning signs that could save lives. They also serve as a motivational tool, helping users to track fitness goals and stay active, promoting better overall health.

Beyond personal health, wearables also gather data that healthcare professionals can use to make more informed decisions. This real-time data gives doctors a comprehensive view of a patient's health history, allowing for more accurate diagnoses and more effective treatments.

India has emerged as a global leader in leveraging technology for healthcare, with a series of innovations. One such breakthrough is the Aadhaar-enabled health infrastructure, which links millions of citizens to a unique identification system, enabling seamless access to medical records and personalised healthcare services. The country is also making strides in AI-driven diagnostic tools, such as Artemis, which assists doctors in detecting diseases like cancer and tuberculosis with unparalleled accuracy. By combining telehealth with mobile diagnostic tools, healthcare providers extended care to regions with limited infrastructure, ensuring no one is left behind.

Telemedicine platforms surged during the COVID-19 pandemic, proving invaluable in maintaining access to healthcare while minimising exposure risks. India pioneered the use of telemedicine in rural areas through platforms like eSanjeevani, connecting patients in remote locations with doctors in urban centres, offering consultations for a wide range of conditions. India is also advancing the field of predictive healthcare with the use of machine learning models to analyse vast amounts of medical data, predicting disease outbreaks, chronic conditions, and even individual health risks. Notably, platforms like HealthifyMe use AI and machine learning to predict and track lifestyle diseases such as diabetes and obesity, providing real-time, actionable health advice tailored to the individual's behaviour and habits.

The adoption of electronic health records has also changed how we store or share medical information. EHR systems centralise patient data, making it accessible to authorised providers across different facilities. This not only improves care coordination but also reduces redundant tests and procedures. EHRs have also opened the door for personalised medicine. By analysing a patient's genetic, clinical, and lifestyle data, healthcare providers can develop tailored treatment plans that maximise effectiveness while minimising side effects.

Robotic surgery has revolutionised how certain surgical procedures are performed. Using robotic arms controlled by surgeons, procedures are more precise, minimally invasive, and result in smaller incisions, which leads to faster recovery times. Robotic surgery allows for greater flexibility, enhanced dexterity and improved visualisation, making complex surgeries safer and more efficient.

In addition to performing delicate surgeries, robots are also being used for routine tasks like sterilisation and delivering supplies within healthcare facilities. This reduces the burden on healthcare staff and increases efficiency, especially in busy hospitals. Robotic technologies are also being used in rehabilitation and elderly care. Robots equipped with sensors and AI can assist patients with mobility exercises, monitor their health, and provide companionship, addressing both physical and emotional needs.

One of the most promising aspects of technology is its potential to accelerate advancements in regenerative medicine.

While these advances have brought numerous benefits, they also raise important questions about their impact on human biology, particularly concerning brain development, cell growth, and hormonal balance. Understanding these effects is essential for managing the long-term consequences of our increasing reliance on technology.

Neurons, the fundamental building blocks of the brain and nervous system, are responsible for transmitting signals throughout the body. The development of neurons is a complex process that begins early in life and continues throughout adulthood, especially in response to environmental stimuli and experiences. Technology has the potential to influence this process in both beneficial and detrimental ways.

The widespread use of wireless technology — smartphones, Wi-Fi, and Bluetooth devices — has led to continuous exposure to electromagnetic fields (EMFs). Research on the biological effects of EMFs is ongoing, with some studies indicating that prolonged exposure to high levels of EMFs contributes to oxidative stress, a process linked to ageing and chronic diseases. However, the overall impact on human health remains an area of continued study, as individual responses to EMF exposure can vary. As technology advances, understanding its long-term effects remains crucial, particularly in relation to brain function and cellular health.

Technology also influences the endocrine system responsible for hormone production and regulation. The hormonal changes driven by our interactions with technology can have wide-reaching effects on mood, stress, and overall health. The impact of technology on human biology is multifaceted, affecting brain development, cell growth, and hormonal balance in profound ways. While there are clear benefits, such as improved medical technologies and tools for managing health, there are clear risks associated with them, too. Understanding and managing these impacts is crucial for maintaining healthy brain development, cell function, and hormonal regulation in the digital age.

The question of equitable access also remains critical. As healthcare systems adopt cutting-edge technologies, it is vital to ensure that advancements benefit all segments of the population, not just the privileged few. The convergence of emerging technologies such as 5G, virtual reality (VR), and genomics will continue to drive innovation in healthcare. VR, for instance, is already being used for pain management, surgical training, and therapy for mental health conditions like PTSD and phobias.

The potential of technology in healthcare is boundless, but its success hinges on collaboration between technologists, healthcare providers, policymakers, and patients. By prioritising innovation, equity, and ethical practices, the partnership between technology and healthcare can pave the way for a healthier, more inclusive future.

The Digital Parent

In previous chapters, I've explored a lot about the mind, particularly the young, developing mind — and let's be honest, there's only so much we can do with an adult brain that's already been shaped, influenced, and, in many ways, corrupted by life's experiences. But when it comes to young minds and future generations, the possibilities are far greater.

That's where real change happens. That's where we have the opportunity to nurture, guide, and protect minds that are still forming — before they become trapped in cycles they never chose.

Parenting in the 21st century is a journey unlike any other. For parents, the technological world offers unprecedented opportunities for learning, connectivity, and creativity, as well as unique challenges. The ways in which parents guide their children in this digital age can shape not only the lives of their children but also the society they grow into. For parents, raising children requires a careful balance between embracing technology and mitigating its risks.

This chapter explores the dynamic relationship between parents and children in a world defined by rapid technological advancement, such as fostering digital literacy, online safety, and nurturing emotional well-being.

Parents now face the responsibility of managing their children's screen time, online interactions, and exposure to digital content. Apps, video games, and social media platforms are all part of a child's daily routine, and parents must navigate the potential risks of cyberbullying, inappropriate content, and online predators.

Simultaneously, technology has opened up new opportunities for education. Educational apps, websites, and games can provide children with engaging learning experiences outside of traditional classroom settings. Parents can use technology as a tool to enhance their children's education, helping them to explore subjects, develop new skills, and engage with their peers in a virtual space.

Technology has permeated nearly every facet of family life - from toddlers learning their ABCs through educational apps to teenagers engaging with peers on social media platforms; children are immersed in technology from a young age. While technology can offer immense educational benefits, foster creativity, and connect families across distances, it also poses risks such as excessive screen time, exposure to inappropriate content, and cyberbullying.

But before we get into technology and parenting, let's just understand a child's brain development journey. This subject is quite new to me too.

Per the experts, the human brain, a marvellously complex organ, begins its formation shortly after conception. This makes a child's brain development one of the most captivating and dynamic processes in human biology. The brain develops at an astonishing pace of 100 billion neurons during early childhood, laying the groundwork for learning, memory, and behaviour. These neurons form the structural foundation of the brain but require connections, called synapses, that occur at an extraordinary rate during early childhood stages. Understanding these stages of brain development and their potential influence in the digital age is crucial for shaping a better society.

We all know that brain development begins in the womb, where the neural tube forms around the third week of pregnancy. By the end of the first trimester, the basic structure of the brain is in place. Proper nutrition, avoiding toxins, and maternal health become crucial to ensure optimal brain development.

The early years, especially up to age 3, are characterised by rapid synaptic growth. During this period, a child's brain produces more synapses than it needs - a process known as synaptic overproduction. These connections are refined through 'pruning,' a process where unused synapses are eliminated, strengthening the ones that are most frequently used. It's important to note that this process is heavily influenced by the child's environment and experiences.

Experts have created the following stages of brain development that help identify what children need at each stage to thrive.

Infancy (0-12 Months): In infancy, sensory experiences dominate as babies process sights, sounds, and touch, forming the foundation for later learning.

Toddlerhood (1-3 Years): n this stage, language and motor skills flourish as toddlers gain independence, explore their surroundings, and form basic social relationships.

Preschool Age (3-5 Years): This is a critical period for language, problem-solving, and social skills. Children learn through play, interaction, and structured learning environments.

School Age (6-12 Years): The brain continues to grow and refine its connections, focusing on logic, memory, and academic skills.

This makes it critical to understand how technology and devices may interact and influence these stages. While the effects of technology on older children and adults are widely studied, its influence on early stages critical for cognitive, emotional, and social development raises unique questions.

The pervasiveness of technology in modern households has introduced interesting dynamics, prompting both opportunities and concerns.

The first year of life is critical for forming secure attachment bonds between family and infants. This stage is vital, and any parental distraction due to excessive use of smartphones or other devices can reduce the quality of parent-infant interactions.

Studies have observed that "technoference" (interference caused by technology) leads to diminished responsiveness to infants' cues. Infants rely heavily on face-to-face interactions for language acquisition and emotional development. Reduced eye contact due to parental device usage may impair these processes.

One of the most debated aspects of technology's influence on infancy is the impact of screen time. While the American Academy of Paediatrics (AAP) recommends avoiding screen exposure for children under 18 months (except for video chatting), the practical reality often deviates. Prolonged screen exposure during infancy is associated with delayed language development and reduced attention spans. Infants learn best from direct human interaction, which screens cannot replicate.

The toddlerhood stage allows for rapid growth in cognitive, emotional, and motor skills. This stage is critical to cognitive development. Toddlers tend to learn better when they are actively involved. Keeping that thought in mind, some companies have created apps that allow children to directly interact with content. Despite that, reliance on technology can hinder cognitive development.

The American Academy of Paediatrics (AAP) emphasises the importance of face-to-face interactions and hands-on play for toddlers. Passive consumption of content, such as watching videos and gaming, can lead to reduced attention spans and limited problem-solving skills.

Recent studies have suggested that overstimulation from fast-paced or highly engaging digital content can make it challenging for toddlers to manage their emotions in slower-paced, real-life complex situations as they grow up, as their brains have already adapted to the technology.

Considering digitisation, the pre-school age is the right time to introduce technology to children slowly. Even though technology's influence on preschoolers' social skills is double-edged. Interactive games and video calls enable young children to communicate with peers and family members, fostering a sense of connection. Yet, concerns about diminishing face-to-face interactions remain. Early childhood is a critical period for developing empathy and social skills through play, facial expressions, and tone of voice. Over-reliance on screens may reduce opportunities for these interactions, leading to challenges in understanding social cues and building relationships.

For school-age children, technology can be a powerful tool for collaboration. Group projects, digital whiteboards, and communication apps allow children to work together, even across distances. Gaming platforms also foster teamwork and problem-solving, particularly in multiplayer settings. However, the rise of social media and online gaming introduces risks such as cyberbullying, social comparison, and reduced self-esteem. The pressure to maintain an idealised online presence can affect children's mental health, highlighting the importance of digital literacy education and parental supervision.

Attention-Deficit/Hyperactivity Disorder (ADHD) is a neurodevelopmental condition characterised by symptoms of inattention, hyperactivity, and impulsivity. The disorder affects millions of children worldwide, often continuing into adulthood. Children with ADHD may struggle with focusing on tasks, managing their emotions, and controlling impulses, which can interfere with their academic, social, and personal lives.

Aggression, defined as behaviours intended to harm or intimidate others, can be a standalone issue or a symptom exacerbated by underlying conditions such as ADHD. The prevalence of digital devices has dramatically increased screen time among children. Studies suggest that excessive screen time can aggravate ADHD symptoms in various forms, including digital aggression and digital fatigue.

Overstimulation: Digital content, especially fast-paced games and videos, can overwhelm a child's sensory processing abilities, intensifying difficulties with focus and impulse control.

Sleep Disruption: Excessive use of screens, particularly before bedtime, can disrupt sleep patterns and, in turn, worsen attention and emotional regulation problems.

Reduced Attention Span: Interactive digital media, while engaging, often reinforces instant gratification and fragmented attention spans, making a child's brain adapt, making them less patient and impairing the prefrontal cortex, affecting decision-making and self-control in the long run.

Children who spend excessive time on digital devices often show reduced attention spans and struggle with concentration. This phenomenon, sometimes referred to as "digital distraction," occurs because constant exposure to fast-paced media conditions the brain to expect immediate gratification, making it harder to focus on slower-paced tasks like reading or problem-solving.

One of the most apparent effects of technology on children is its impact on physical health. The sedentary lifestyle associated with excessive screen time has led to a significant rise in obesity rates among children. According to research, many children spend hours engaged with screens—television, tablets, smartphones, or gaming consoles—leaving little time for physical activity. This lack of movement contributes to poor cardiovascular health, weak muscle development, and an increased risk of chronic diseases like diabetes.

Furthermore, prolonged use of screens is linked to vision problems such as digital eye strain, dry eyes, and near-sightedness. Children often use devices at close range for extended periods, exacerbating these issues. Poor posture during device use, such as slouching or craning the neck, can also lead to musculoskeletal problems like back and neck pain.

Additionally, reliance on technology for answers can hinder critical thinking and problem-solving skills. When children turn to search engines or educational apps for instant solutions, they may miss out on the deeper learning that comes from grappling with challenges. Moreover, excessive screen time can negatively impact academic performance, as children may prioritise digital entertainment over homework and study.

Children engrossed in their screens may miss opportunities to interact with family members or peers, leading to feelings of isolation and loneliness. Many children are exposed to violent video games, movies, or online content, which can desensitise them to violence and promote aggressive behaviour. Moreover, excessive screen time limits opportunities for unstructured play, where children invent their own games or explore their environment. This lack of hands-on experience can hinder their ability to think innovatively and adapt to new situations.

The pervasive presence of technology strains family relationships. Many parents report feeling "disconnected" from their children. Shared family activities, such as meals, conversations, or outdoor play, are often replaced by individual interactions with digital devices. This lack of quality time together can weaken family bonds and reduce opportunities for parents to model positive behaviours or guide their children's development.

I remember one Indian phrase, "Yatha pitaro lokah", meaning as parents, we shape our children's understanding of the world, so we must lead by example in everything we want them to do.

Children learn by example, and in today's hyper-connected world, this includes how parents engage with technology. If a parent is glued to their phone or tablet or uses the devices to entertain themselves, it sends a clear message the same exact message to a child. Many parents themselves are engrossed in technology and like it to make their lives convenient and sophisticated but often forget how it impacts their children's development. We share online jokes with our kids, giving them the impression that online presence is a good source of information and fun. We forget that children's brains are not yet fully formed, at least until the age of 12. They simply accept this as a good thing and get used to the technology.

To set a good example, parents must model balance and awareness in their use of technology. It's important to consider the devices brought into the home, as they can impact a child's perception. For an adult, sensor lights are a practical way to save energy and enhance safety, but for a child, they're nothing more than a fun game, shaping their view of technology as pure entertainment with little understanding of its practical value or the need for balance.

Being present during family time, such as meals or conversations, is another way to demonstrate the importance of connection over digital distractions. Relationships between couples, prioritising face-to-face interaction, unplugging during specific times, and showing the children that there's a life beyond screens can instil the same habits in kids.

While technology enables families to connect with people outside the home, it often has the opposite effect, causing family members to retreat into their digital worlds. Family time, conversations, and play are essential for childhood development, helping to foster creativity and social skills. However, digital devices often offer passive entertainment, such as watching videos or playing pre-designed games, which can stifle creativity and limit opportunities for imaginative thinking.

Cloudy Bonds

Talking about adult relationships, like many aspects of life, technology has transformed these too, giving rise to what I call "cloudy bonds." These bonds, much like clouds, can often feel ephemeral, delicate, and difficult to grasp. Formed and nurtured primarily in the virtual realm, these bonds have become an essential part of human interaction today.

At their core, these bonds represent interpersonal connections forged through digital platforms — whether social media, chat rooms, dating apps, or online communities. Unlike traditional associations that emerge through face-to-face interactions, digital bonds rely on text, voice, video, and other digital media. Each online bond is unique, affecting individuals in its own way and shaping the evolving landscape of human connection. While some of these digital bonds may eventually transition into in-person connections, they still alter our way of thinking and interacting with one another.

Social media platforms like Facebook, Instagram, and Twitter have revolutionised how we stay connected with friends, family, and acquaintances. These platforms often centre around sharing life updates, photos, and experiences, fostering a sense of connection. As these online interactions transition into in-person connections, the perceptions formed through digital interactions play a significant role.

Since our brains have already constructed a mental image of the person based on their online presence, we tend to view them through that lens. This pre-existing perception then continues to influence how we interpret their behaviours and interactions in the real world, sometimes aligning with reality but at other times creating discrepancies.

Online dating has become a mainstream way for people to meet potential partners. Apps like Tinder, Bumble, and more allow individuals to connect based on shared interests, values, and preferences. As per the makers of these apps, these platforms provide an opportunity for people to find love across geographic boundaries. In some cases, online relationships might develop into deep, meaningful partnerships, but the anonymity of the digital world can also lead to deceit or misrepresentation. Research has shown that online relationships are one of the biggest factors in the decline in human trust.

Online networking platforms like LinkedIn have revolutionised the way people build and sustain professional relationships. They provide an accessible space for connecting with colleagues, mentors, and industry peers, making it easier than ever to expand professional networks. While these connections often lead to valuable opportunities and collaborations, they can sometimes feel transactional or impersonal, with networking taking precedence over fostering authentic human interaction.

The internet also allows people to connect in specialised forums or support groups, offering a sense of community for individuals facing specific challenges (mental health, addiction, chronic illnesses, etc.). These digital spaces can provide invaluable support, validation, and information. However, the anonymity of these online relationships can sometimes create challenges with trust and accountability, and emotional support may not always be as fulfilling as face-to-face interactions.

While online relationships have their drawbacks, they also provide significant benefits in our modern world. They help transcend borders, connecting individuals across continents. Often offering a degree of anonymity and allowing individuals to express themselves freely. Interactions can occur at different times, providing flexibility in communication. These relationships are not limited to romantic bonds; they encompass friendships, professional connections, and communities formed around shared interests.

Individuals can connect regardless of physical limitations, disabilities, or societal constraints. Marginalised communities, such as LGBTQ+ groups, find safe spaces to interact and form meaningful relationships. Online platforms often allow users to construct and share their identities in ways that may be difficult offline.

While cyber relationships have helped many people and increased connectivity, recent research suggests that their challenges and disadvantages are slowly beginning to outweigh the benefits. Some key concerns include:

Mental Health Concerns: As individuals become more entrenched in online relationships and digital worlds, issues like anxiety, depression, and loneliness are on the rise. The constant pressure to present an idealised image of oneself online, coupled with the loneliness that often accompanies superficial connections, is contributing to an increasing mental health crisis.

Impact on Real-World Relationships: Online connections erode the quality of physical-world relationships. Any connection is built on effort, dedication, and mutual partnership. Bonds are also built rather than matched. Technology creates an illusion that relationships are easy. The abundance of options in the online world has created a "swipe" culture, where users quickly move from one profile to another, often resulting in people feeling unsatisfied with any one person, always wondering if there might be someone better just a swipe away.

Redefining Intimacy: As digital interactions become more sophisticated, the traditional concept of intimacy is evolving, sparking debates about authenticity. I always argue that we only have and will always have 24 hours a day. On average, an individual spends about 8 hours working, 8 hours sleeping, and about 2-3 hours on daily tasks, such as travelling, cooking, grooming, etc. That leaves about 5 hours or so in a day. Add an hour or two for yourself, leaving 4 hours or less to spend quality time with your loved ones! Now, imagine dividing these 4 hours between your partner, family, friends (online and offline) and other networking. How would you prioritise!

In relationships - whether with a partner, family, or friends—time is a critical component. Without it, relationships wither. In particular, family relationships, as they are the most critical ones, require the most time. Forget building a new relationship, even to maintain existing relationships; I argue that 4 hours or less a day is not enough. Emotional intimacy requires vulnerability, trust, and shared experiences, none of which are easily facilitated by the fast-paced nature of swipe culture.

Digital Dependency: The reliance on cyberspace for relationships is posing a serious threat of individuals losing the ability to engage offline. A heavy reliance on technology for emotional support weakens people's ability to develop and sustain real-world connections and friendships. Over time, this contributes to a sense of emotional detachment.

Digital Deception: The anonymity and flexibility of the internet often enable individuals to misrepresent themselves. Catfishing - where people create fake profiles to deceive others - continues to be a significant concern. We are already seeing a rise in the use of artificial intelligence to create highly convincing virtual personalities. These AI-generated personas could lead individuals into relationships with entities that aren't real, blurring the lines between humans and machines.

Trust in another Human: Digital communication, such as emails, messages, or even video calls, lacks the non-verbal cues of body language, tone of voice, and intentions. This leads to misunderstandings and misinterpretations, fostering scepticism in society.

Recently, several videos have surfaced featuring company CEOs instructing and addressing employees, but these videos have been revealed to be fraudulent. Both the video and audio content are entirely AI-generated, creating a misleading and deceptive representation of reality.

Online interactions often prioritise the number of connections over their depth. Social media platforms encourage users to accumulate friends and followers, fostering a sense of achievement rooted in quantity rather than meaningful engagement. This superficial focus can paradoxically lead to feelings of loneliness and dissatisfaction, even while being "connected" to hundreds or thousands of individuals.

Consider this: How many LinkedIn connections do you have? And how many of those people do you truly know as individuals, beyond their professional profiles?

Cyberspace relationships are undoubtedly a testament to humanity's ability to adapt and innovate in the digital age. One of the most profound ways technology has changed family dynamics is through its impact on communication and its effect on work-life balance. Remote work, facilitated by email, video conferencing, and cloud-based collaboration tools, has allowed parents to better manage their time and reduce the time spent commuting. This flexibility can have a positive impact on family life, as parents are able to spend more time at home, attend their children's events, and participate more fully in family activities.

The COVID-19 pandemic accelerated the widespread adoption of remote work, and many companies have continued offering flexible work arrangements even as the pandemic receded. Parents working from home can now be more present for their children during the day, participate in household chores, and better manage their work schedules. Flexible hours and the ability to work remotely have made it easier for parents to juggle family responsibilities while maintaining their careers.

However, the boundary between work and family life has also become increasingly blurred. The constant availability of work-related emails, messages, and tasks can create an environment where it becomes challenging to disconnect and focus entirely on family. Parents working from home may struggle with the temptation to keep working during family time, while children may feel that their parents are always busy with technology, creating a vicious cycle.

This increased technological advancement also raises concerns about privacy and over-parenting. The ability to constantly monitor children's activities can lead to a loss of autonomy for kids, potentially creating tension between parents and children.

The diminishing quality and quantity of relationships in today's world is another complex issue influenced by technology, social norms, and changing lifestyles. While modern life offers many conveniences, it also presents significant challenges for individuals seeking to form meaningful, lasting connections. To counteract this trend, it is important for individuals to make a conscious effort to prioritise relationships, spend time together offline, and communicate more openly and authentically. Building and nurturing strong relationships - whether with family, friends, work, or romantic partners - requires effort, vulnerability, and a commitment to genuine emotional connection.

Ultimately, the goal must be to cultivate meaningful, authentic connections that enrich our lives, both online and offline. In a world where technology constantly evolves, it is all too easy to become swept up in the rush of virtual interactions. However, true connection transcends screens and clicks. As we continue to navigate the complexities of the digital era, striking a balance between the advantages of technology and the pitfalls of superficial interactions will be essential.

Remember, it's not about how many connections we have, but how deeply we understand, empathise, and truly see one another—how we share our fears, our joys, and our authentic selves without hesitation.

Let's not allow technology to turn our already fragile connections into something even murkier and cloudier. Instead, let's use it as a bridge to transform distant, untouched, surface-level bonds into profound, genuine relationships.

Forget not: Even connections that start online can evolve into something real, dissolving the fog of superficiality and bringing clarity and depth to our human experience.

Technology: A Boon and A Curse

We cannot deny the transformative power of the digital age, but so are the challenges it presents. The dichotomy of technology as both a boon and a curse underlines its multifaceted impact.

A study by the National Institute of Health (NIH) concluded that there needs to be more awareness of the dangers of technology, especially in an age where technology is required for many of our daily obligations.

The advancement of technology has made the world a global village. Instant messaging, video calls, and online tools enable seamless communication across time zones, fostering global connections and collaborations.

Businesses thrive on technology-driven communication, enhancing productivity and reducing cost or geographical barriers. Social media platforms allow individuals to share their lives, promote causes, and build communities.

However, these advancements have their pitfalls. The constant connectivity often leads to information overload, digital fatigue, and dependency. Social media, while enabling connection, can foster misinformation, cyberbullying, and unhealthy comparisons. Furthermore, concerns about digital privacy loom large. Personal data is often exploited by corporations, exposing users to risks such as identity theft and intrusive advertising.

Despite these advances, technology has not bridged the gap for all. High-tech medical solutions are often expensive, limiting access for underprivileged populations. Over-reliance on technology raises concerns about errors in automated systems. Ethical issues, such as genetic engineering and data privacy in medical records, spark debates about the implications of unchecked technological growth in healthcare.

Technology has contributed significantly to environmental monitoring and conservation. Satellite imagery aids in tracking climate changes, while smart technologies optimise resource consumption in homes and industries. Renewable energy technologies, such as solar panels and wind turbines, offer sustainable alternatives to fossil fuels.

On the flip side, technological advancement often comes at an environmental cost. The production and disposal of electronic devices contribute to pollution and e-waste. Mining for rare earth metals, essential for modern devices, damages ecosystems and depletes finite resources. Energy-intensive technologies, such as cryptocurrency mining, exacerbate the global carbon footprint.

Modern technology has created a climate where online behaviours can have immense mental health consequences offline. From sitting in front of screens for work to using screens for escapism and entertainment, we are increasingly experiencing phenomena like burnout, technology addiction, and brain rot.

Brain rot is a relatively new issue researchers are studying that is caused by constant engagement with social media, online videos, video games, television, and other forms of screen time. The incessant use of technology and high screen time can overstimulate our brains and lead to serious mental health issues. According to the Forbes Coaches Council, the way we interact with each other and our perceptions of reality have dramatically shifted because of the effect of technology on our thinking.

Buying and selling things, dating, planning a doctor's visit, and even waiting in line have changed. As a result, our approach to the world and ourselves has taken an entirely new form, and we're constantly inundated by new information. Through our 24-hour news cycle, an endless feed of text and images, and an unending exposure to celebrity and influencer culture, our ways of thinking have been undeniably linked to technology.

FOMO, or the fear of missing out, is another psychological, social, and technological phenomenon where users experience severe mental health consequences like anxiety, lower self-esteem, and depression because of content posted on social media. In other words, users feel FOMO when they see friends or followers post content that excludes them, which only further exacerbates feelings of isolation. Behavioural addictions related to social media are gaining attention in psychological circles as people find it more difficult to disconnect from technological opportunities around them.

The International Journal of Environmental Research and Public Health claims that both extroverts and introverts are developing addictive practices because of easy access to social networking sites (SNSs). The report found that the more people are engaged with social media in unhealthy ways, the more likely they are to have lower academic achievement, lower job performance, and greater real-life relationship problems.

Gambling addiction has always been a serious issue, but like many other addictions, it has been enhanced by the internet's ease of access. Both websites and smartphone apps allow users to make bets with real money on virtual poker games, lotteries, sports games, and more.

Much like gambling addiction, addiction to pornography has become more of a problem in the digital space. Accessing pornography is easier than it's ever been, and it increases the risk of developing an addiction.

The overuse of social media, binge-watching on streaming platforms, and excessive online gaming can also contribute to a symptom researchers call numbing. Numbing may serve multiple psychological functions, such as replacing emotional regulation skills and distracting from stress or uncomfortable feelings.

Technology numbing is a cognitive and emotional response to the overexposure of digital devices, screens, and the constant flow of information. It can be understood through the lens of psychology, neuroscience, and behavioural science.

At the neurological level, technology numbing affects the brain's reward system. When we engage with digital devices, particularly social media, our brains release dopamine, a neurotransmitter associated with pleasure and reward. This creates a cycle of seeking instant gratification as we become accustomed to the quick bursts of dopamine. Over time, this leads to an increased need for constant stimulation, which may desensitise us to the point where we require more extreme or frequent engagement with technology to achieve the same emotional response.

Researchers explain this numbing response as an action of our sympathetic nervous system. In the face of physical or emotional pain or a traumatic incident, our sympathetic nervous system has three responses: fight, flight or freeze. Emotional numbing is freezing. Our brain shuts down as a protective response to keep us safe when our nervous system is overloaded.

This response is a form of dissociation, which we get by avoiding complex feelings and escaping into the digital space. Whether our escape is social media, constantly finding new people, streaming platforms, gambling, or pornography, access to our phones often feels like a more comfortable alternative than facing our feelings and putting the work in to improve our mental well-being.

What's Next?

As humanity stands on the brink of a great breakthrough driven by our mastery of technology, and after decades of hype, artificial intelligence is showing signs that it might be close to reaching human levels of intelligence; the obvious question that comes to mind is – where we will go from here!

Quantum computing and big data analytics offer the tantalising prospect of solving some of life's most profound mysteries, from the existence of extraterrestrial life to the inner workings of the human brain.

Artificial intelligence is improving through learning, and machines are becoming more cognitive. In 1997, Deep Blue, an IBM supercomputer, beat the legendary chess player Garry Kasparov in a six-game series. It was a major step forward for artificial intelligence. But it was possible because chess is a relatively finite game based on clear rules. Teach a machine the rules, and we can teach it to win. So far, artificial intelligence has been good at performing individual tasks like playing chess. But it hasn't yet learned to replicate wider human intelligence effectively.

Things that come naturally to us, like intuition or creativity, remain difficult for machines. That said, this has now started to change, as the game Go shows us. Go is a marvellously intricate two-player board game in which players strive to encircle more territory than their opponent. A chess game has an average of 35 possible moves at any given time. In Go, this number skyrockets to 250. The Go grid boasts 361 squares, compared to chess's 64, and an astonishing 10 to the power of 170 potential board configurations.

That's too many to really comprehend, but for perspective, it's far more than the number of atoms in our universe. So, when someone plays Go, they rely more on human intuition and feeling than logical, rule-based decisions. It just isn't possible to do all the calculations. This reliance on human intuition makes Go a unique and deeply human game.

That's why when AlphaGo, an artificial intelligence created by Google's DeepMind, beat Lee Sedol, a top player in the game, it was clear that we were on the cusp of major advances. But how did AlphaGo succeed? Well, DeepMind gave it a collection of 30 million moves collected from human players and then trained it to play.

The machine was programmed for reinforcement learning, mimicking a human brain. That meant that artificial intelligence collected points when it did something that proved correct and lost them when it made mistakes. Then, DeepMind trained AlphaGo against different versions of itself. Each time it played a game, it would learn by remembering which move brought it a reward, creating a cycle of improvement.

Observers of AlphaGo commented that its moves were inventive, with seasoned players even describing some as divine!

Clearly, machines are becoming more human, developing intuition and creativity - even though it's not true intuition and creativity like humans, as it is still human-trained and data-fed. In some instances, we have trained machines enough to teach themselves continuously by using and refining data – but we cannot ignore the fact that the shift is getting faster.

Nanotechnology is tiny, but it will be the next big thing to change our lives. Pluck a single hair from the head. It's not very wide, is it? But in nano terms, it's huge.

A single nanometre is about one ten-thousandth of its width. That's the kind of scale we're talking about when we talk about nanotechnology. One of the most promising aspects of nanotechnology is its potential to enhance our health. Nanomaterials can possess greater strength and less weight, but the most intriguing application of nanotechnology is its ability to enhance our bodies. Advancements in computing and sensors at the nanoscale mean we will soon be able to combat diseases and maintain our health with the aid of nanorobots. Envision a future where nanorobots constantly monitor our circulatory system, ready to fight viruses, bacteria, and other disease-causing agents. Roaming inside our bodies, they will be able to attack viruses, bacteria, and other disease-carrying bodies. For example, researchers have developed a nanotechnology delivery system for an anti-cancer agent called tumour necrosis factor alpha. The system's nanorobots would float through the bloodstream, dispensing the agent when required and evading the threat of any pathogens seeking to attack them. Nanotechnology will also help us manage long-term conditions. Patients with diabetes might soon have nanorobots in their bloodstream, constantly measuring their blood nutrient levels and giving them a boost of the right chemicals at the right time. In Indian mythology, the gods sailed the oceans searching for an elixir of immortality.

Some have speculated that COVID-19 vaccinations were an early test for nanotechnology, with claims of post-vaccination changes in the mind and body. Whether there is any truth to this remains to be seen.

The Greeks talked of an elusive elixir of life. Well, maybe we're about to stumble across a modern-day panacea in the form of nanotechnology that gives us the power to control our health. Combine that with the power of genetic coding, and we have the power to play God. That makes this world so dangerous. We forget that, ultimately, we are mere humans. We forget that we have limited understanding and limited brains. We know that whenever humans have tried to play God, we have only ended up destroying more than creating. Let's hope that with true awareness and knowledge, we can cultivate balance.

Humanity must develop clear guidelines and ethics for artificial intelligence, but doing so is also not easy. In March 2018, an autonomously driven Uber vehicle hit and killed a woman, making her the first pedestrian to be killed by a self-driving car. This immediately raised a difficult question.

Who is to blame in this case? The owner for owning the car and using it for its intended purpose? The manufacturer of the car? The company that built the software that controls it.

As smart machines become more and more a part of our daily lives, the question of how we regulate and control them becomes greater. Some of these are practical questions. For instance, how do we prevent robots from being hacked and misused?

IOactive, a firm of security consultants, has demonstrated how real this risk is by hacking into and taking control of Alpha 2, a humanoid robot designed to be a household assistant. They instructed it to pick up a screwdriver and repeatedly stab a tomato. Then what about morals?

Should we encode them into robots? If so, whose morals?

Science fiction offers a good starting place for considering this question. The famous science fiction writer Isaac Asimov proposed, as long ago as 1942, three laws for robots. First, a robot must not injure a human or allow one to come to harm. Second, a robot must obey its orders, except where they would conflict with the first law. Third, a robot should protect itself as long as that protection does not go against either of the first two laws. These three laws are a good start, but they provide no clear guidance for some of the thorny situations a machine might face.

Consider again a self-driving car that sees a pedestrian step out unexpectedly into the street. It has to make what is essentially a moral choice. It can swerve dangerously to protect pedestrians but risk its owner's life. Or it can prioritise its owner's safety at the expense of the pedestrians. Does a self-driving vehicle have a loyal duty to protect its owner? And if so, do taxis and public transit vehicles behave differently from privately owned cars? And should a vehicle's calculations change if the pedestrian is a child or an elderly person? Sure, it will take some time for us to come to grips with questions like these.

Anyways, we've explored some of the problems our technological revolution is throwing up. Now, let's consider some of the excitement that awaits us.

Technology may help us solve the mystery of whether we are alone in the universe. There are around seven sextillions, or ten to the power of 21, stars in the whole universe, each with its own planets, just like our sun. Do we really believe that intelligent life has evolved nowhere else but here?

It's statistically likely that life exists elsewhere in the universe. But if that's the case, why haven't we encountered it? One theory is the zoo hypothesis, formulated in 1973 by astronomer John A. Ball. According to Ball, one or more alien societies exist. It's just that they're watching us from afar as we observe animals in a zoo. In this theory, extraterrestrials are intelligent enough to recognise an independent natural evolution and sensitive enough not to disturb it. If that seems unlikely, consider that we try to allow tribal peoples such as the Jarawas in the Indian Andaman Islands to live undisturbed by contact with modern societies.

Another theory is that we simply wouldn't recognise contact if it were made. According to the famous whistleblower Edward Snowden, all intelligent societies come to encrypt their communications. It may be, he argues, that alien messages are out there, but we are incapable of telling them apart from the background noise of cosmic radiation. The good news, however, is that our advances in science and technology may mean that we're getting closer to solving this mystery. The Breakthrough Listen Project at the University of California, Berkeley, is dedicated to listening for extraterrestrial communication.

In 2015, an artificial intelligence project was used to analyse cosmic noise picked up on a series of repeated radio bursts coming from a galaxy 3 billion light-years from Earth. It was thought at first that these bursts resulted from a catastrophic event like the death of a star. However, the bursts appeared again in both 2016 and 2017. That means that whatever caused them had lived on. Scientists believe that the source could be an extraterrestrial intelligence that existed 3 billion years in the past, a time when we were just single-celled organisms. That huge gulf of time between us points to the fact that even if we ever saw extraterrestrial life, we might not recognise it.

Life on different planets may no longer resemble life as we understand it. These beings might have merged their biology with technology, resulting in life forms that exist only as information. That, after all, may very well be the next step in our own evolution. And it could happen sooner than we think.

The singularity is coming, and it may leave us immortal or extinct. The concept of the singularity has captivated the imaginations of futurists, technologists, and philosophers alike. Often referred to as the Technological Singularity, it represents a hypothetical point in the future where technological growth becomes uncontrollable and irreversible, fundamentally transforming human civilisation.

The futurist Ray Kurzweil takes more vitamins and minerals than an average 70-year-old, popping around 200 pills a day. Why? Well. He believes that by the middle of this century, humans will become immortal. And naturally, he's determined to still be alive at the time. Kurzweil isn't some old crank but a recognised expert in artificial intelligence, the future, and the singularity. Kurzweil predicts the singularity will come in 2045.

We can't know for sure. One rather bleak possibility is our extinction. How could that happen? It could be a simple mistake. Consider a medical artificial intelligence designed to eradicate cancers that decides that the best way to do so is to eliminate the host, humans.

But it's not all bleak. As legendary physicist Stephen Hawking has said, the singularity could be the worst thing to happen to humanity, but it could also be the best.

That's because it offers the tantalising possibility of immortality. Transhumanists believe that singularity will advance our understanding of the human brain so far that we will be able to achieve digital immortality as our bodies become temporary vessels for our digitalised minds, which will be stored in the cloud. At present, we don't understand enough about how the physical cells of the brain become our conscious mind for this to be achievable. However, Hawking believes that the brain is essentially a computer and that, therefore, it will be possible one day to copy it and provide life after death. Ray Kurzweil has noted that in the future, we will be able to send millions of nanobot scanners through each capillary of our brain to scan every neural feature. Take into account the vast, rapid advances in nanotechnology, artificial intelligence, and data analysis that the singularity would bring, and living as an immortal digital consciousness doesn't seem so unlikely after all.

While experts differ on the timeline, the rapid advancements in AI research point to the possibility of superintelligence within this century, if not sooner. AI today has already made significant strides, as I have mentioned in this book. However, these are narrow AIs designed to excel at specific tasks. Superintelligence, on the other hand, would involve a system with general capabilities that are able to handle a wide range of challenges across different domains without human intervention.

Superintelligence refers to a form of artificial intelligence that exceeds human intelligence in virtually every domain, from problem-solving and creativity to social interactions and strategic thinking. It is often depicted as an AI that can autonomously learn, adapt, and innovate beyond human limitations. This level of intelligence could revolutionise industries, healthcare, technology, and education.

Given the potential for both positive and negative outcomes, ensuring the safe development of superintelligent AI require careful planning, regulation, and international cooperation. Researchers, policymakers, and technologists must work together to create ethical guidelines, regulatory frameworks, and safety protocols for the development of AI. Countries will need to establish global agreements and regulatory bodies, like the one I have mentioned in this book, to manage the risks associated with superintelligence.

Today, we are essentially the same beings as our earliest ancestors who wandered the plains of Africa. But after a time, everything will change. We may look at Homo sapiens and its intelligence as we today look back at Neanderthals. Ahead of us lies a great rupture in human existence and the possibility of a new, superintelligent species. So, for now, keep taking those vitamins…. Or perhaps, rely more on the human instinct!

Future of Human instinct in the Digital Age

Often, it feels like the modern world is already a kind of sci-fi fantasy. Who'd have thought that one day, we could ask household gadgets to play a song, delegate our fridge to prepare our shopping list, or, indeed, have a watch to remind us of when it's time to go for a walk or when to drink water?

But this is just the beginning. The development of deep learning and natural language acquisition is turbocharging AI innovations. Autonomous cars and weapons are already in development, and deepfake videos and virtual reality games are becoming so convincing that it's hard to distinguish fiction from fact. With that, the obvious question is what the future of human instinct will be in the coming days. Let's look at it with a short fictional story about what the world could look like in 2045, that is, after another 20 years of development, followed by an analysis of the impact these developments could have on us.

In Mumbai, India, in 2045, Neha's family dramatically lowered their insurance premiums by signing up with a new insurance company called Ganesh Insurance. But with a catch. They had to agree to share all their personal data with the company. Ganesh instructed the family to use a certain set of apps for everything from investing to finding the best supermarket deals.

And over the next few weeks, their phones were constantly pinging with recommendations. The apps told them when to drink water, instructed her father to drive more slowly, and nagged her brother so much about his eating sweets that he eventually quit. With every healthy decision they made, their insurance premiums fell. It seemed like a win-win for everyone.

But when Neha's daughter fell in love with a man who lived in a less wealthy neighbourhood, the family's premiums soared. Somehow, the AI had inferred that he was of a different social status and interpreted that as a health risk to the family.

In short, AI can help optimise our lives, but it can also weaponise the data. The story provides a chilling insight into how AI can reproduce the discrimination already present in society. One of the most significant AI developments in the last decade has been deep learning. Deep learning allows computers to make predictions, classify data, and recognise patterns. Facebook uses this technology to generate personalised recommendations and maximise the time we spend on its network. By analysing every click we make and comparing the data to the millions of others in their system, the platform is able to accurately predict what will engage us. Deep learning can have enormous benefits. AI can analyse millions of data points and make connections that would elude the human mind. But AI lacks the nuance and complexity of human thinking. It can't draw on personal experience, abstract concepts, or common sense and is vulnerable to bias and discrimination.

In this story, the app didn't know that the love interest was from a different caste and that the match would be seen as socially undesirable. However, by analysing his family's data and tracking where he lived, it could still be suggested that the match would be a threat to the health of another family.

Deepfake is a term that may not be widely known today but is projected to pose a significant threat by 2045. Consider a scenario where a dubious company approaches you, an esteemed health expert, to misuse your skills to create a deepfake video. They request a video of a prominent politician confessing to scandalous behaviour. If you decline, the company could resort to releasing a fake video depicting you in a compromising situation at a nightclub. And it's already happening now. In 2018, a video of former President Obama calling President Trump a total dipshit went viral online, causing an uproar. The catch? It wasn't real.

It was a deepfake created by BuzzFeed to show what was possible with AI technology and to warn people to be sceptical of what they see. To develop the technology for making deepfakes, developers first needed to teach computers to process and make sense of images. So, they took inspiration from the human brain, which has a visual cortex that gathers information about an image before sending it to the neocortex, which processes that information and then assigns more complex meaning to what's being seen.

Using this model, designers created a Convolutional Neural Network or CNN. To create deepfakes, we need a specific kind of technology called a Generative Adversarial Network, or GAN, which consists of two CNNs. One of these is a forger, which analyses tens of millions of pixels in every image it sees, picking out the unique characteristics of every image.

If the forger has analysed images of, say, dogs, it can then synthesise a fake dog image. It sends this to the second CNN in the network, which is a sort of detective. It tests fake pictures against real ones and informs the forger of any errors. The forger then uses that feedback to improve the image and sends it back to the detective. This cycle recurs millions of times until the fake dog is indistinguishable from the real one – a process that can create very convincing deepfake videos and images, with dangerous consequences.

This will only grow more prevalent and powerful in the years to come. How to make it beneficial to society as a whole will be one of our most urgent preoccupations in the near future. How can we continue to enjoy technology's convenience without becoming technology-dependent?

The answer lies in balance, which begins with self-awareness. By recognising how and when technology affects well-being, we can make informed choices about how to interact with it.

Affective computing is an interdisciplinary field at the crossroads of computer science, psychology, and cognitive science, dedicated to developing systems that can recognise, interpret, and respond to human emotions. As artificial intelligence (AI) grows more sophisticated, affective computing is reshaping human-computer interaction (HCI) by adding an emotional layer that enhances user experience, decision-making, and communication.

The term refers to technologies that sense and simulate human emotions. It goes beyond traditional machine learning by incorporating insights from emotional psychology, biometrics, and computational modelling—bridging the gap between human emotions and digital systems. At its core, affective computing equips machines with emotional intelligence, enabling them to recognise, interpret, and respond to human emotions. This involves leveraging sensors, machine learning algorithms, and psychological models to process affective states. Examples include facial recognition software that detects micro-expressions, wearable devices that monitor physiological responses like heart rate or skin conductivity, and natural language processing tools that analyse tone and sentiment in voice or text

About eight years ago, I came up with an idea that was ahead of its time. Imagine walking into a restaurant after a long, exhausting day. Maybe work drained you, or you had a frustrating argument with your boss. Now, instead of flipping through a generic menu, I present you a menu that provides food that directly changes your emotional state using a system that would capture emotional data.

The idea wasn't just about food—it was about creating a personalised dining experience using cutting-edge emotional analysis

- **Facial Expression Analysis:** Cameras and computer vision algorithms analyse micro-expressions and facial movements to infer emotions.
- **Speech Emotion Recognition:** Acoustic features like tone, pitch, and rhythm are processed to detect sentiment.
- **Physiological Signals:** Wearable devices monitor heart rate, skin conductivity, and brainwave patterns to infer emotional states.

Once the system collected this data, advanced models—neural networks, fuzzy logic, and statistical analysis—would classify emotions into categories like happiness, anger, sadness, or neutrality. The restaurant would then adapt accordingly. A virtual waiter might use a soothing tone when detecting stress, while the menu would adjust recommendations based on biochemical responses.

Feeling anxious? A dish rich in magnesium and Omega-3s could naturally calm your nervous system.

Mentally drained? A serotonin-boosting meal packed with complex carbs and tryptophan could help restore your mood.

Need confidence before a big meeting? A dopamine-enhancing dish might be just what you need.

A place where psychology, emotions, and culinary science come together to transform how we interact with what we eat. Because food isn't just fuel; it's emotion, memory, and medicine.

But when I first proposed this idea, it was rejected. Some dismissed it as too ambitious, others failed to see its potential. Perhaps the world wasn't ready. Perhaps the technology wasn't advanced enough at the time.

Or maybe—just maybe—this was a door that was never meant to be opened. After all, the very technology that could enhance trust and well-being is also the same technology that fuels surveillance, privacy concerns, and emotional manipulation. Was this kind of sensory tracking a step toward progress, or just another layer of the vicious cycle we find ourselves trapped in today?

This for sure requires a bit more research and understanding.

Affective computing is more than a technical breakthrough—it's a step toward humanising technology. What makes us truly human isn't just intelligence but the intricate balance of multiple forms of it—Intelligence Quotient (IQ), Emotional Quotient (EQ), Social Quotient (SQ), and Adversity Quotient (AQ).

IQ is the simplest form of intelligence, not unique to humans. Ants, chimpanzees, and other mammals exhibit problem-solving abilities, strategic thinking, and even collective decision-making. This is why many argue that what sets us apart isn't just a high IQ, but the depth of our emotional, social, and adaptive intelligence.

So far, we have only been able to artificially replicate fragments of this knowledge. Not that we haven't tried to merge all four into machines—but thank God, we've failed. And in that failure, we have preserved what makes us human, resisting the temptation to play God.

Yet, as machines inevitably gain more emotional intelligence and the lines between humans and machines blur, a deeper question emerges: *How much should technology truly understand us?* And more importantly, once it does—*who will be in control?*

While affective computing promises more natural, intuitive interactions, it also opens the door to unprecedented influence over human emotions.

Yet, hope remains.

Human emotions are deeply rooted in biochemistry, driven by neurotransmitters like dopamine, serotonin, oxytocin, and cortisol. These chemicals influence mood, motivation, and stress levels. By understanding these biochemical mechanisms, affective computing can influence emotional states, fostering well-being and productivity, such as,

Stress Reduction: Virtual therapy applications can use affective computing to detect signs of anxiety or stress through voice or facial cues.

Mood Enhancement: Entertainment platforms can analyse user preferences and current emotional states, offering content that stimulates dopamine release, enhancing enjoyment and engagement.

Social Connection: Robotic companions in healthcare settings, such as eldercare, can be designed to foster oxytocin release through empathetic interactions.

Learning Optimisation: Adaptive educational technologies can identify when learners are frustrated or disengaged. By intervening with encouragement or tailored challenges, they create a positive learning environment that boosts serotonin levels.

If developed ethically and responsibly, affective computing could transform human-computer interaction (HCI) into something truly meaningful - where technology adapts to us, rather than the other way around.

The future of affective computing is not just about innovation; it's about responsibility. The real question is not whether machines will understand us, but whether we will still understand ourselves in a world where they do. In teaching machines to understand emotions, we must ensure that we don't sacrifice what makes us uniquely human.

In our pursuit of progress, we must continually ask: **At what cost?**

With imperfect humans, there is always the risk of mistakes—but also the hope of wisdom, compassion, and accountability. The challenge remains to strike the right balance, ensuring that in making machines more human, we don't end up making humans less so

A Growing Divide

Another important aspect that we must be aware of and control is ensuring that technology does not increase the disparity between those who can afford the latest technological advancements and those who cannot. Technology should be accessible to everyone, regardless of their financial status, and not create a divide that has significant implications for individuals, communities, and nations.

As the world continues to embrace the digital age, a significant digital divide is emerging between urban and rural communities, as well as between wealthy and low-income populations.

Recently, I fell sick. I was alone and unable to find the strength to go outside, so I got the idea to order it via an app. Within 30 minutes, I had the medicine, some flowers and fresh food delivered to my doorstep. Amazing. Isn't it? One of my friends said, *"so thankful that these apps exist today"*. I couldn't agree more with them at that time.

A few days later, I was passing by a medicine shop, and I realised that the retail price of the same medicine and flowers that I ordered online was different in the shop. Now it wasn't like a convenience fee or delivery fee that inflated the price on the app, but the price itself was different on the app vs in the shop. Again, this diminishes trust but also creates a world that is not equal.

I am lucky enough to be able to afford an inflated price. But is that fair? Is that fair to a person who really needs medicine but cannot afford that inflated price? Does this not create a digital divide in society?

The digital divide refers to the gap between individuals who have access to modern information and communication technology (ICT) and those who do not. This divide is often influenced by factors such as income, geography, education, and infrastructure. As technology continues to advance, this gap is widening, with wealthy individuals and nations able to access the best tools and resources while others are left behind. It's the same discussion as recently could have been witnessed in COP29.

In many parts of the world, particularly in developing countries or rural areas, access to technology is limited or non-existent. For example, in some rural areas, reliable internet access may be a luxury, preventing residents from taking advantage of online education, remote work opportunities, or even basic healthcare services. Similarly, high-end devices such as smartphones, laptops, or tablets remain unaffordable for large segments of the population, effectively shutting them out of the digital world.

This digital inequality undermines the very promise of technology—that it can improve lives, create new opportunities, and enhance human potential. As technology evolves, it is crucial to ensure its benefits are distributed equally across society, not just concentrated in the hands of a few who can afford it.

From education to healthcare, technology is a tool that can bridge gaps, create new avenues for growth, and enhance personal and collective development.

Education is one of the most powerful tools for breaking the cycle of poverty, and technology plays an increasingly vital role in making it more accessible. Online learning platforms, digital textbooks, and virtual classrooms have the power to democratise education, allowing students from different parts of the world to learn from the best institutions and instructors, regardless of their geographic location. However, for this to become a reality, universal access to technology is crucial.

For instance, during the COVID-19 pandemic, the sudden shift to remote education revealed the disparities between students with access to high-quality devices and internet connections and those without. In affluent countries, students continued learning seamlessly with the help of high-speed internet and laptops, but in low-income communities, many children were left behind due to the lack of access to such resources. This issue highlights a growing concern in both the West and the developing world: digital learning cannot replace the traditional classroom experience unless every student has the same access to the necessary tools.

For instance, in the U.S. and UK, the issue of *digital equity* has been a pressing concern. Government efforts, such as the *E-rate programme* in the U.S. or broadband expansion initiatives in the UK, aim to ensure that underserved communities can access affordable broadband. But even in these developed nations, gaps persist, particularly among marginalised communities. In India, rural schools may not even have proper classroom infrastructure, let alone the ability to access high-quality virtual learning.

In countries like India, government initiatives like *Digital India* aim to bridge this divide, but the challenge remains steep. While the expansion of mobile networks has helped millions of Indians access the internet, the cost of data plans and the lack of affordable devices can still be significant barriers. The government is working to provide cheaper data plans, but the underlying issue remains that digital infrastructure is often concentrated in urban centres, leaving rural populations disconnected.

Technology is also transforming healthcare. Telemedicine, AI-powered diagnostics, and wearable health devices are revolutionising the way people access medical services. In remote areas, telemedicine allows patients to consult doctors without travelling long distances, saving time and money. AI technologies can diagnose diseases more accurately and quickly than traditional methods, potentially saving lives.

However, these advancements are not universally available. People in lower-income areas often lack access to healthcare technologies that could improve their health outcomes. By making these technologies affordable and accessible to everyone, we can ensure that healthcare services are not a privilege of the few but a right for all.

In the modern economy, digital skills are increasingly essential for finding a job or advancing in one's career. However, not everyone has access to the tools or training necessary to acquire these skills. For example, in many underprivileged communities, people may not have the resources to purchase computers or take online courses to build technical skills. As a result, they are excluded from the digital workforce and unable to access the economic opportunities that technology provides.

In contrast, those with access to technology can enhance their skills through online courses, freelancing platforms, and remote work opportunities. These individuals are better positioned to participate in the global economy, which increasingly relies on digital proficiency. To create an equitable workforce, access to technology must be extended to everyone, enabling individuals to develop the skills necessary to thrive in the digital age.

Technology moves forward because of innovation, and innovation thrives when people from all walks of life bring their unique ideas to the table. But if technology is only in the hands of a select few, we miss out on countless creative solutions — ideas that could tackle some of the biggest challenges we face, from climate change to social inequality. These aren't issues one person, one company, or even one country can solve alone. Real change happens when technology is accessible to everyone, sparking collaboration and fresh thinking. When more people are involved, innovation doesn't just serve a privileged few — it works for society as a whole.

Technology has the power to change lives — but its benefits shouldn't be reserved for those who can afford it.

In India, we say "Vasudhaiva Kutumbakam" — the world is one family. If we truly believe in this, we must build systems, policies, and infrastructure that ensure everyone has access to technology, not just a privileged few. Because when knowledge and tools are shared, innovation flourishes, communities thrive, and we create a society that uplifts all, not just some.

As the Greek philosopher Aristotle once said, *"Educating the mind without educating the heart is no education at all."* The same applies to technology—advancement without inclusivity is no true progress. When we make technology accessible to all, we don't just create a smarter world—we build a fairer, more connected, and truly innovative future.

A Clarion Call for Action

As technology evolves, three outcomes are inevitable:

- The development of technology and AI. The momentum behind research and innovation is unstoppable, driven by both commercial and political competition.
- AI will eventually surpass human intelligence. As machines continue to learn and improve, they'll outpace human cognitive abilities.
- Mistakes will occur. The introduction of such power is bound to come with errors, and these could lead to significant challenges, especially if AI begins to act in ways that aren't aligned with human interests and instincts.

These risks highlight the need for ethical frameworks to guide AI development. The path we choose now will determine whether AI becomes a tool for enhancing human life or a force that we struggle to control.

We stand at a critical crossroads where rapid technological advancements. Such as, artificial intelligence, robotics, blockchain—can either uplift humanity or deepen inequality, erode ethical foundations, and disrupt societal harmony. This is a clarion call for action—a collective effort that bridges the gap between technological progress, human well-being, and sustainable growth. Rooted in the universal values of compassion, equity, and shared responsibility, and inspired by the Indian ethos of interconnectedness, we must act decisively. The path forward demands systemic changes, inclusive governance, ethical leadership, and a steadfast commitment to ensuring that innovation fosters a future defined by harmony, dignity, and shared prosperity. If we fail to act, we risk jeopardising not just technological progress but the sustainable growth and collective well-being of humanity itself.

Here, as part of my urgent call to action for organisations and government policymakers, I propose a path forward that emphasises systemic changes, inclusive governance, and ethical leadership.

Establishing a Global, Unbiased Technology Governance Body

One of the most urgent priorities is the creation of a global, impartial organisation, akin to the United Nations, dedicated to technology governance. This body, tentatively named the Global Technology Ethics and Oversight Council (GTEOC), would serve as a cornerstone for responsible innovation by:

- **Establishing Universal Standards:** Crafting global guidelines for technology development and deployment, ensuring ethical practices that respect diverse cultural and economic contexts.
- **Overseeing AI and Data Usage:** Monitoring the responsible application of artificial intelligence, big data, and emerging technologies to prevent harm, misuse, or discrimination.

- **Mediating Disputes:** Serving as a neutral platform to resolve conflicts related to technological ethics and cross-border data management.
- **Promoting Inclusivity:** Elevating the voices of developing nations and underrepresented communities in critical decision-making processes.

By acting as both a guide and a watchdog, GTEOC would ensure that technological advancements are steered with fairness, equity, and humanity at their core.

Appointing a Chief AI Ethics Officer (CAIEO) in Every Organisation

Technology is no longer confined to the tech industry; it permeates every sector. To ensure ethical alignment, organisations must embed ethical oversight within their leadership structure. The creation of a Chief AI Ethics Officer (CAIEO) role is a critical step forward.

- Ethical Risk Assessment: Evaluate the ethical implications of AI and technology projects before and during deployment.
- Bias Detection and Mitigation: Develop frameworks to identify and reduce algorithmic biases, ensuring equitable outcomes.
- Compliance and Transparency: Ensure adherence to legal, ethical, and organisational standards, while promoting transparency with stakeholders.
- Training and Advocacy: Foster an organisational culture of ethical awareness through training programs and workshops.

By institutionalising the CAIEO role, organisations can proactively address the ethical challenges posed by technological innovations.

Emphasising Technological Literacy for All

To bridge the gap between technological advancements and human understanding, we must make technological literacy a priority.

Education systems, workplaces, and communities must take an active role in ensuring individuals are equipped with the skills and awareness necessary to navigate an increasingly digital world. This means empowering people to:

- Understand the basics of emerging technologies—how they work, how they evolve, and how they impact various aspects of life.
- Identify potential risks and benefits of digital tools—so that individuals can make informed decisions rather than passively adapting to technology-driven changes.
- Critically evaluate the ethical dimensions of technology—from privacy concerns and algorithmic biases to the societal consequences of AI and automation.

This isn't just about keeping up with technological progress; it's about ensuring that humans remain in control of it.

Innovating with Purpose

Innovation must be rooted in purpose. It's not just about what we can create but why we create it. Companies, governments, and researchers must shift from innovation for the sake of progress to Purpose-Driven Innovation — a framework that ensures technological advancements are aligned with addressing real, pressing global challenges such as climate change, inequality, and healthcare.

For instance:

- Climate Tech: Innovation should focus on reducing carbon emissions, promoting sustainability, and building climate-resilient infrastructure.
- Healthcare Innovations: AI and emerging technologies can be leveraged to improve diagnostic accuracy, optimise treatments, and increase healthcare access in underserved regions.
- Equity-Focused Solutions: Most importantly, technology must work for all, not just the privileged. This means designing solutions that

empower marginalised communities, close socio-economic gaps, and ensure digital inclusivity. From affordable Ed-tech solutions to financial tools for the unbanked, innovation must uplift rather than exclude.

Building Ethical Supply Chains

Technological advancements are only as ethical as the supply chains that support them. Yet many of these supply chains remain opaque, unregulated, and, at times, exploitative. From rare earth minerals mined under harsh conditions to factories with poor labour practices, the human and environmental cost of innovation is often hidden behind layers of complexity.

To build a more ethical and sustainable technological future, companies must take practical steps to ensure that their supply chains reflect the same values of transparency, fairness, and sustainability that they claim to champion. This means:

- Blockchain for Transparency: Use blockchain technology to create transparent supply chains that track the origin and impact of raw materials and components.

- Fair Labour Practices: Partner only with suppliers that adhere to ethical labour standards, ensuring fair wages and safe working conditions.

- Circular Economy Models: Design products with recyclability and sustainability in mind, reducing electronic waste and environmental harm.

The future of humanity and technology are deeply intertwined. To ensure this relationship remains symbiotic rather than exploitative, we need to consider decisive, practical measures. Concepts such as establishing unbiased governance structures like GTEOC, institutionalising ethical oversight through mechanisms akin to CAIEOs, fostering technological literacy, prioritising purpose-driven innovation, and creating ethical supply chains are ideas I propose as a starting point—though the specifics may evolve, similar initiatives must take shape.

This is not merely a call for balance; it is a call for action. The decisions we make today will define the legacy of the digital era. Let us strive to leave behind a legacy of empowerment, equity, and enduring human connection—a future where uncertainty gives way to intentional, ethical progress.

Conclusion

Today, here we are, swept up in the grand, dramatic swirl of progress—carried away by the unstoppable tide of technology and gadgets galore. What once seemed neat and manageable has now exploded into sprawling, tangled mazes that influence every little corner of our lives. So, here's the big question: *have we let loose a beast we can no longer control*? And if we have... well, what exactly do we do about it?

Ah, *balance,* my trusty magic bullet. Toss it around like we've cracked the code to life. But let's be honest. Is it the answer? Well... yes and no.

As someone aptly pointed out to me, balance isn't truly a solution unless we first understand what balance really means. Balance isn't a trophy we earn once and proudly display forever; it's more like an endless treadmill — one where we're always moving while carefully monitoring our heart rate and every other little signal our bodies are sending us.

When it comes to navigating the modern age wisely, the balance lies in untangling the complex and often uneasy interplay between *self-awareness, convenience, and control* — a dynamic that has quietly shaped societies for generations.

Of these, self-awareness remains the most misunderstood. It's not just about controlling our thoughts or knowing when to switch off a device. True self-awareness involves an ongoing dialogue between two vital aspects of ourselves: the inner child and the inner parent. The two parts often tug at each other, creating a delicate balance that profoundly shapes how we experience and respond to the world. For example, when we feel the urge to scroll mindlessly through our phones, it might be our inner child craving a moment of escape or joy. At the same time, the inner parent may nudge us to put the device down, recognising the need for rest or focus.

Beyond this interplay, self-awareness is also about tuning into our neurochemicals and noticing the sensations within our bodies. Every sensation carries a message—every minute, every moment. Yet, we rarely pause to pay attention, let alone truly listen. Let me illustrate this with an example.

Imagine you're baking a cake. Every ingredient plays a role, and you can observe and feel the process unfold: the sweet aroma of vanilla sparks your senses, kneading the dough makes your arms ache, and tasting the batter excites your taste buds. Each step elicits a distinct physical reaction.

Understanding how neurochemicals manifest physically requires us to tune into specific bodily signals, which are often clear and measurable if we pay attention. Neurochemicals don't just influence our emotions; they also trigger tangible, physical reactions that can serve as signals for what's happening in our brain and body.

Take dopamine, the "reward" chemical. When it surges, we might feel a lightness or energy boost, often with a tingling in the limbs or a quickened heartbeat. Imagine finishing a challenging task at work—can you feel that warmth in your chest or the faint smile only you notice?

Cortisol, the stress hormone, is often easier to detect. A spike might make palms feel clammy, muscles tense, or breathing shallow. For instance, during a high-pressure meeting, you may notice a tightness in your traps or an increased sensitivity to noise.

But it's important to remember that each of us may experience slightly different physical sensations. Let me give you an example: one day, after spending too much time thinking and writing this chapter, my eyes grew tired, my limbs ached for movement, and my lips became dry. These simple physical reactions were my body's way of telling me that my brain had been overworking and that I needed to slow down.

For precise self-awareness, you can take it a step further by pairing these observations with data.

For example:

- Notice how your heart rate changes.
- Monitor changes to body temperature, as it may rise slightly during a dopamine surge or drop with oxytocin release.
- Observe breathing patterns — stress tends to shorten and quicken breaths, while relaxation extends and deepens them.

And No. You don't need a device to observe these. It's critical to notice these on your own. To train and initially understand these sensations, for sure, you can take the help of a psychologist or trained professional.

Humans are hardwired for connection. From the moment we're born, we're driven by an innate need to bond with others, to be seen, heard, and validated. These deep, primal human instincts fuel everything from our social interactions to the way we engage with the world around us.

In the past, our instincts were triggered by real physical threats, such as predators. Today, it's technology that sets off those same responses. The problem: Our brains can't always distinguish between real and reel.

When we think about reducing tech's negative effects, we think "keep the phone away" or "try a digital detox." Sure, those things help, but let's be real—they're not enough. How can we expect a real break if we're still filling our homes with gadgets in the name of growth and convenience?

Think about it: isn't it a bit naïve to believe that keeping a phone out of reach when still wearing a computer tracker on our wrist as we sleep? It's like locking the door but leaving the windows wide open.

That's why it's more important than ever to take a step back and do a reality check. Pause and reflect before being tempted by the latest gadget or technology.

It's time to rethink what 'progress' and 'convenience' really mean. And most importantly, what it truly means to be 'human.

Parents today juggle concerns like educational apps, games, and AI, which excite kids but can also make them dependent on technology. With more single parents and nuclear families, devices have become the go-to babysitter. It feels good knowing kids are engaged, but we often forget — technology doesn't just entertain. It rewires their brains.

The real issue isn't tech itself; it's how we engage with it. Gadgets aren't the enemy, but their impact depends on how we use them. Here's the kicker — alongside screen time, we need to nurture critical thinking. And by that, I mean the ability to think before we search.

These days, the default response to any question is, *"I'll check it on Google."* But when every answer is just a search away, don't you think we risk losing the ability to question, analyse, and reflect.

We live in a world overflowing with both information and misinformation, and it's on us to teach the next generation how to tell the difference. Because knowing how to find an answer is one thing—knowing if it's the right one is another. AI and tech companies design algorithms to tap into our primal instincts—the dopamine rush from social media, or the fear sparked by sensational news. But what we often overlook is a simple yet powerful truth: every algorithm follows one basic rule—I keep serving you what you like, but every now and then, I'll throw in something from the adjacent area.

Unfortunately, our world operates on maximisation. We chase massive goals. To achieve massive goals, we maximise revenue. And to maximise revenue, we maximise attention—because attention drives everything.

And what's the easiest way to grab attention? Outrage. *"Did you know? Did you know? Did you know?"*

A constant flood of shocking headlines, half-truths, and algorithm-driven noise—designed to feed us knowledge, information, and wisdom. But does knowing everything really make us wiser?

Or, in the race to stay ahead, do we forget that the wiser one is not the one who knows it all—but the one who knows what to know and what not to know?

The future we build depends on our understanding of ourselves. Fostering self-awareness and integrating technology in ways that complement us, not complete us, we can truly go places. We must ensure that the tools we create enhance our lives without eroding what makes us human.

The digital world mirrors our values, biases, and priorities—much like a child. It's essential that we lead by example, embodying kindness, empathy, and ethical conduct—both online and offline.

The success of digital platforms, products, and experiences is shaped by human preferences and behaviour patterns. At the core of it all, we each face a choice—do we maximise the *product* (make something better that genuinely benefits people), or do we maximise *profit*?

History shows that when profit takes priority, quality often takes a backseat. There's even a name for this phenomenon—*Gresham's Law*—which suggests that bad speech drives out good speech.

This is why the field of Digital or Cyberpsychology is so essential—it helps us understand the profound impact technology has on our thoughts, feelings, and behaviours. By gaining a deeper understanding of these effects, we can make more informed choices and create a healthier, more balanced world.

Because in the end, even as the digital world evolves at lightning speed, one truth remains: humans are the heart of its creation, governance, and future. AI and automation may redefine possibilities, but human ingenuity, ethics, and vision still shape its direction.

So yes, even in this digital age, *human instinct matters* more than ever. And as we innovate, we must never lose what makes us human—*our ability to empathise, to reason, to tell stories*, and, most importantly, *to make choices based on more than just dat*a.

As I sit here, typing these final words, I realise that even I am not immune to the pull of the digital world. I check my notifications more often than I should. I sometimes scroll mindlessly. I have, at times, let algorithms shape my thoughts without even realising it.

But here's the thing—now, I catch myself. I pause. I question. I choose. Because knowing is the first step towards choosing. And choosing—that's where change begins.

www.ingramcontent.com/pod-product-compliance
Lightning Source LLC
Chambersburg PA
CBHW031119020426
42333CB00012B/143